GOD'S HARP STRING

D1731661

GOD'S HARP STRING

The Life and Legacy of the Benedictine Monk

Swami Abhishiktananda

Edited by William Skudlarek OSB

Lantern Books • New York
A Division of Booklight Inc.

2010

LANTERN BOOKS
128 Second Place
Brooklyn, NY 11231
www.lanternbooks.com

Copyright © 2010 Monastic Interreligious Dialogue

All rights reserved. No part of this book may be reproduced, stored in a retrieval system, or transmitted in any form or by any means, electronic, mechanical, photocopying, recording, or otherwise, without the written permission of Lantern Books.

Printed in the United States of America
Cover photograph by Christoph Baumer

LIBRARY OF CONGRESS CATALOGING-IN-PUBLICATION DATA

God's harp string : the life and legacy of the Benedictine monk Swami Abhishiktananda / William Skudlarek, editor.

p. cm.

ISBN-13: 978-1-59056-181-2 (alk. paper)

ISBN-10: 1-59056-181-3 (alk. paper)

1. Abhishiktananda, Swami, 1910–1973. 2. Monks—India—Biography. 3. Hinduism—Relations—Christianity. 4. Catholic Church—Relations—Hinduism. I. Skudlarek, William.

BX4705.A214G63 2010

261.2'45092—dc22

[B]

2010007079

Contents

Monastic Interreligious Dialogue and the Abhishiktananda Society

Monastic Interreligious Dialogue

Monastic Interreligious Dialogue (MID) is an organization of Benedictine and Trappist monks and nuns committed to fostering interreligious and intermonastic dialogue at the level of spiritual practice and experience between North American Catholic monastic women and men and contemplative practitioners of diverse religious traditions. Its current president is Father Mark Serna of Portsmouth Abbey, Portsmouth, Rhode Island.

MID in North America is one of several regional commissions that have been formed by Catholic monastic communities throughout the world to promote interreligious dialogue. The work of these commissions is coordinated by a General Secretariat established in 1994 by the Abbot Primate of the Benedictines acting in agreement with the Abbots General of the two branches of the Cistercian order. It is currently headed by Father William Skudlarek OSB of Saint John's Abbey, Collegeville, Minnesota.

In order that the dialogue of monks and nuns be in explicit communion with the universal Church, the General Secretariat ensures contact with the Pontifical Council for Interreligious Dialogue.

THE ABHISHIKTANANDA SOCIETY

The Abhishiktananda Society was formed by friends and disciples of Swami Abhishiktananda five years after his death in 1973 to promote the publication of his writings and to make available, for the first time, his spiritual diary and the articles and essays that had not been published during his lifetime. Another goal of the Society was to encourage the dialogue and the spiritual meeting between different religious traditions—Hinduism and Christianity in particular.

Even before it was legally formed, the Society began publishing an *Occasional Bulletin*, later known as *SETU*. Because of legal complications, but also because many felt that its principal objectives had been accomplished, the Society was dissolved by its board of directors in 2008.

INTRODUCTION

To mark the one-hundredth anniversary of the birth of Henri Le Saux, the French Benedictine monk who was one of the great pioneers of interreligious dialogue, The American Commission of Monastic Interreligious Dialogue (MID) presents this collection of articles selected from its *Bulletin* and from the *Occasional Bulletin* (later known as *SETU*) of the now extinct Abhishiktananda Society.[1] MID is especially grateful to Dr. Bettina Bäumer, past President of the Society, for her help in determining which articles to include and for providing invaluable editorial assistance.

Le Saux was born on August 30, 1910, in Saint-Briac, a coastal town in Brittany. In his late teens he entered the monastery of Sainte Anne in Kergonan, also in Brittany. Nineteen years later, on August 16, 1948, a day after the first anniversary of India's independence, Le Saux arrived in Madras and made his way to Trichy in the southern state of Tamil Nadu to join Jules Monchanin, a priest from Lyons who was convinced that the Catholic Church in India had to become Indian in its theology, worship, and life. In 1960, they founded the Saccidananda Ashram—more commonly known as Shantivanam—in a mango grove on the banks of the Kavery River, about fifty kilometers from Trichy.

Le Saux left his monastery in France to bring Benedictine monasticism to India. Within the space of a few years, however, he had become so taken by the power, beauty, and truth of Vedantic spirituality, especially in its non-dualistic expression (*advaita*), that he became a *sannyasi*, taking the name Abhishiktananda. He spent most of his remaining twenty-five years in India wandering about in his saffron robes and plunging ever more deeply into the spiritual wellsprings of the Vedas and Upanishads.

Swami Abhishiktananda was more of a spiritual seeker than a systematic theologian. However, throughout his years in India he struggled to reconcile his new spiritual experiences with the doctrinal tradition of Christianity. It may still be too early to give a final assessment of his success in establishing a meeting point between his *advaitic* sense of God's oneness with the self and the Church's trinitarian, Christological, and soteriological doctrines. There can be no doubt, however, about the sincerity of Abhishiktananda's search for God—the ultimate vocation of the Catholic monk—and his courage in following that search wherever it took him, no matter the cost.

The year 2010 will see a number of conferences and symposia to clarify and assess the spiritual and theological legacy of Swami Abhishiktananda. The first was held in January at the ashram he and Jules Monchanin founded, and its proceedings will be published by Lantern Books. Other publications—new editions of Abhishiktananda's own writings, books about him, and the proceedings of other conferences—will surely appear in print and online. May this modest collection of articles be a way of whetting the appetite for the banquet that will soon be served.

William Skudlarek OSB
Secretary General, DIMMID

PART ONE

PERSONAL RECOLLECTIONS
OF SWAMI ABHISHIKTANANDA

An Interview
with Odette Baumer-Despeigne

Pascaline Coff OSB

Sister Pascaline Coff is a member of the Benedictine Sisters of Perpetual Adoration. She was one of the founders of the North American Commission of Monastic Interreligious Dialogue and served as its Executive Secretary for many years. Madame Odette Baumer-Despeigne carried on a lengthy correspondence with Abhishiktananda and met him in the last months of his life. Until her death in 2002, she worked tirelessly to make him known and have his writings published. This chapter first appeared in number 51 (October 1994) of the Bulletin *of the North American Commission of Monastic Interreligious Dialogue.*

*S*wami Abhishiktananda was living in India the last decades *of his life. You, Odette, were in Switzerland. What brought about your meeting with Swamiji?*[1]

That's a long story! As regards non-Christian religions, my own inner journey began sixty years ago. At the time I was brought up in a convent in Belgium. Among the subjects taught was, of course, religion. At the end of one year's lectures on the Mystery of the Holy Trinity, given by a well-known theologian of the day, his concluding words were, "I have taught you all that can be known about God's mystery." My reaction was immediate: if at the age of seventeen I already knew all that one could know about God, what was I to do all my life? And I began to weep.

Fortunately, the next year our teacher was a university professor from Louvain, a Jesuit who lectured on the then-new science, missiology. He began with these words, which pierced through the depths of my heart: "In missiology one has to begin with a study of the great world religions, so I am going to introduce you to those religions existing outside Christianity." From that very second I knew what I was going to do all my life! He gave us the rudiments of Hinduism and Buddhism. Alas! The nuns found this way of teaching much too revolutionary and he stopped coming. The excuse: "He no longer had time."

But for me it was enough; a direction had been given to me: the study of non-Christian religions. So as soon as I left the boarding school I entered the School of Philosophy and Religion of Louvain University, for I felt the need to deepen my own Christian roots to begin with.

Ten years later I had the good luck to meet Abbé Jules Monchanin who was on the eve of his departure for India where he wanted to live out "in silence and complete poverty a contemplative life of study and prayer, while adopting the Hindu monastic way of life." In 1956, I came across a book called *A Benedictine Ashram* written by him together with Père Henri Le Saux. I was thrilled!

A few years went by and in early 1965 (I was then living in Switzerland) I followed a series of lectures given by a learned Hindu monk. Upon discovering the Eastern way of thinking and the Upanishadic spirituality, I was confronted with many questions raised by my Christian faith. This was another milestone in my life.

Fortunately, my guardian angel was keeping vigil and made me successively discover Raimundo Panikkar's book *Essay in Dialogue Between World Religions* and Henri Le Saux's original French version of *Saccidananda: A Christian Approach to Advaitic Experience.*

At once I wrote to Father Le Saux, asking him to help me sort out the different challenges I was now facing. His answer came by return mail and was very encouraging. I corresponded with him for seven years, from 1966 until his death. I received seventy-eight letters, all referring to spiritual matters. At long last I went to India in 1973, planning to meet him on the banks of Mother Ganges. But, alas!, his heart attack hindered me from seeing him in his beloved surroundings. So we met face to face and heart to heart in a hospital room. My presence here today is the consequence of that encounter, seven weeks before his "great departure"—his death.

Abhishiktananda arrived in India in 1948. Can you tell us about his life prior to and leading up to his going to India?—his early life and then, as a monk, what led to his decision to live in India?

Henri Le Saux was born in August, 1910, at Saint-Briac in Brittany, France, as the eldest of a family of eight children. His parents had a grocery store. The family atmosphere was conservative middle class. He felt called to the priesthood at an early age; therefore, his parents sent him to the minor seminary, from which he entered the major seminary. In 1924, his mother nearly died in giving birth to a sixth child. The next year, when another child was expected, Henri was anxious about the life of his mother. To his prayer he added a vow that, if everything went all right, he would dedicate himself wholly to the Lord and would accept "to go even to the most distant mission."

Being recognized as a bright student, his superiors wanted to send him to Rome for further studies, but he refused because he felt called to the monastic life. In 1929, at the age nineteen, he entered the Benedictine Abbey of Sainte Anne de Kergonan, where later he successfully filled the posts of librarian and professor of Church history and patristics. As librarian he had ample opportunity to read widely, and felt particularly drawn to the Greek

Fathers. He was especially moved by Gregory Nazianzen's Hymn
to God beyond all Names:

> You who are beyond all, what other name befits you?
> No words suffice to hymn you. Alone you are ineffable.
> Of all beings you are the End, you are One, you are all, you
>   are none.
> Yet not one thing, nor all things. You alone are the Unnameable.

Meeting, so to speak, "the Unnameable" marked a turning
point in his spiritual journey. From then on he began to read every
author who spoke about the apophatic way of approaching God
and whatever he could find concerning India. That is why, in his
first treatise "Love and Wisdom," a study of the dogma of the
Trinity that dates from 1942 and is dedicated to his mother, he
already uses quotations from Tagore's poem "Gitanjali."

This flashing intuition—God is beyond all names—he made
his own; it would accompany him all the way till his death: God is
beyond all mental categories, beyond all conceptualization. From
now on he has only one dream: to realize his vow and go to India.
He had to wait thirteen years before receiving permission to do it.
To prepare himself, he began to learn Sanskrit, Tamil, and English
and to read as much as of the Hindu scriptures as he could find.

In 1945, the Abbot gave him permission to investigate the possibility of realizing his project. He wrote many letters but without
any result. Finally he wrote to the bishop of Tiruchirapalli [Trichy]
in 1947, explaining that he would like to settle somewhere in his
diocese in a hermitage where he could lead a contemplative life, in
the absolute simplicity of early Christian monasticism and at the
same time in the greatest possible conformity with the traditions
of Indian *sannyasa*.

As the letter was written in French, the Bishop asked a French
priest to translate it; it was Abbé Jules Monchanin, who was

working in his diocese and who himself had desired to adopt precisely this kind of life. The bishop agreed to receive Le Saux and have the two French priests live together in the modest presbytery of Kulittalai, which Monchanin had named "Bhakti Ashram."

All the formalities having been fulfilled, Le Saux left his abbey, embarked at Marseille, and reached India on August 16, 1948. The next day Monchanin reported to a friend, "The Benedictine Father has come! I can only praise God.... In essentials—the conception of our mission, understanding of Hinduism and the monastic life—he agrees more than I had ever hoped with what I have always desired."

A few days later Monchanin added, "As days pass in his company, I wonder more and more at the most incredible convergence of Father Henri's ideas and my own aspirations. And this is all the more striking, because at the human level....we are very different." Le Saux, for his part, wrote to his father, "This correspondence in outlook and thought with Monchanin is extraordinary. A providential coming together."

In 1950, they founded the Shantivanam Ashram. Father Le Saux was never again to leave his adopted country; he became a naturalized citizen in 1960. A last and important remark: he kept constant contact with his monastery, of which he remained a monk until his last day. In India he was and is known under his Indian name: Swami Abhishiktananda—Swamiji to his friends.

In your own account of Swamiji's life you quote his reference in a letter to "the tensions resulting from the presence of the Upanishads and the Gospel in a single heart." Can you expand on this struggle a little more for us?

With this question you touch the very heart of our subject: Swamiji's interreligious dialogue on the existential level.

The phrase you quote is from a letter written by Le Saux in 1952 to his friend Joseph Lemarié, monk of Kergonan. At the time,

Le Saux was living as a hermit in a cave on Mount Arunachala. In his letter he describes the confrontation between his Christian experience and the specific Hindu experience on the level of the ground of one's own being. Thus, in Swamiji we witness the encounter of two mysticisms, Eastern and Western, and this not only on the intellectual level, the level of comparative studies, but more deeply on the experiential level—always effected without the least syncretism.

His disciple, Marc Chaduc, said in a poetic way, "Swamiji never ceased to contemplate the Mystery which has a Face even as the Gospel presents it in the person of Jesus, and at the same time the Mystery that has no face as it was revealed in the hearts of India's Rishis, the Sages of yore," an experience which "requires nothing less than the total surrender of the little ego-self to the inner Mystery." Swamiji let these two modes of experience interact with one another in his soul while remaining all the time open to whatever might happen under the shock of their encounter. Therefore, he wrote, "In all my writings all is biographical and nothing is! Everything comes from the experience of this tension, but everything has been rethought by the mind in the halo of a double culture." That is why I want to answer your question, Pascaline, by quoting Swamiji's words as much as possible. The first result of this confrontation was the realization that "it is to the extent that one leads a deep inner life that one will understand India, and be understood by India."

Swamiji realized that he was embarking "on a journey to the unknown." He was reassured when remembering Saint Augustine's words: "Do not go outside; return into yourself; the truth dwells in the inner man." And Saint Paul's affirmation: "The Spirit of God dwells in you" (Romans 8:9).

Barely six months after his arrival in India, in January 1949, Henri Le Saux went to Tiruvannamali with Jules Monchanin in order to meet one of the most authentic sages of modern India, Sri

Ramana Maharshi, who was living at the foot of the sacred mountain of Arunachala. In spite of the fact that this meeting was to be a crucial moment in his spiritual journey, no word was exchanged between them.

In his diary Le Saux says of this meeting, "My mind was carried off as if to an unknown world. Even before I was able to recognize the fact and still less to express it, the invisible halo of this sage was received by something in me deeper than words. Unknown harmony awoke in my heart....it was as if the very soul of India penetrated to the very depths of my own soul and held mysterious communion with it. It was a call which pierced through everything, rent it to pieces and opened a mighty abyss.... The Ashram of Ramana helps me to understand the Gospel; there is in the Gospel much more than Christian piety has ever discovered."

Who was this Ramana Maharshi who impressed Swamiji so much? One could say: a man radiating the bliss of inner peace and freedom. His teaching was very simple. To every questioner he would say: "First ask yourself—Who is asking the question? Who am I who ask the question? First know who is that 'I,' and you will discover that your small ego is not the real Self, not the root of your being."

It is important to underline that this teaching is not only Ramana's personal teaching, but expresses the very core of Hindu spirituality, namely *advaita* (non-duality). There is no two. Being simply is and cannot be divided. From now on Swamiji's spiritual itinerary is firmly established: at any cost, to live in accordance with the presence of the Upanishads and the Gospel in his own heart.

Between 1952 and 1958 Henri Le Saux stayed for long periods in one or other of the caves at Arunachala, living a very strict ascetic life as a Christian hermit among Hindu solitaries. He was faithful to the daily celebration of the Eucharist and recitation of the breviary in addition to long hours of silent meditation. In 1952, he spent five months in *mauna* (total silence). He plunged headlong into the Hindu spiritual experience of non-duality. Right from the beginning he was very well aware that this path would not be an easy one, that he would have to face much suffering in the exploration of the Mystery hidden in the depths of his own soul.

Please do not forget that Henri Le Saux undertook this exploration fifteen years before the Second Vatican Council, and that his personal humanistic background acquired before coming to India was made up of the very classical and strict, narrow scholasticism that was the standard level of his time. Swamiji wanted to undergo this experience "in the name of the Church." His aim was to live his Christian faith together with the insights of the Upanishadic tradition.

At times the struggle made him state, "Alas, I have tasted too deeply of *advaita* to be able to return to the Gregorian peace of the Christian monk. Alas, in the past I have drunk too deeply of that Gregorian peace not to feel a certain anguish in the midst of my *advaita*." A few months later he wrote, "May the Lord have pity on me and end my life. I can't stand it anymore." His anguish attains its apex in 1956 when, referring to Ramana and Arunachala, he writes, "They have become part of my flesh, they are woven into the fibers of my heart." Here in truth we touch the central depths of the interior drama that was played out in his soul as he was torn to pieces between his loyalty to Christ and his overwhelming Upanishadic experience. He writes to his friend Lemarié, "I am afraid, an ocean of anguish wherever I turn. I am afraid of risking eternity for a mirage…yet I have nothing to fear, Christ is my Sadguru, my true guru."

So, for long years Le Saux, without allowing the slightest sign to appear outwardly, continued to be engulfed in torments—until at last the light of peace and the joy of spiritual awakening illuminated his whole being. In reading his diary, one can feel that the tension was especially intense until about 1960. From then on, without resolving the problems intellectually, the inner light of peace increasingly dawns upon him.

Can you share any of the fruits of this "crossing over" and its tension in his twenty-five years in India?

Since Vatican II recognized the existence of religious pluralism, the question of the universal presence of the Holy Spirit who is at work beyond all institutional barriers arose forcefully. In 1982, Archbishop Jadot, President of what was then called the Secretariat for non-Christians in Rome, declared, "Other religious traditions may help us to come to a deeper understanding of all that Jesus has taught us." In the words of Abhishiktananda, "The Christian must seek to discover in himself, in his or her greatest depth, both the experience of non-duality of being which is the ground of the Vedantic experience, and the experience of divine sonship, the ineffable non-duality of the Father and the Son in the unity of the Spirit, which is the basic reality in the Christian faith." To arrive at this discovery, it seemed to Swamiji that there was nothing more appropriate than rumination about the sayings of the Upanishads, which leads to inner silence and beyond, exactly there where the Holy Spirit finds a suitable place to blow.

In Swamiji's words, "It is no joke to descend to the mystery of one's own being, for one fears one's essential mystery. Nevertheless it is important that this be done in the Church in an experience which is real, direct and barren in its nudity, for we are created in God's image and likeness. Christianity is not tied to its Mediterranean expressions."

Time and again, Swamiji insisted upon that point: "The Gospel is not bound to the Jewish world in which it was disclosed. Its universal and ontic value burns and melts the honeycombs of the Judeo–Greek expressions in which this honey is stored. It is the very echo of the human heart, the message of love, of mutual giving, of relationship in the world. The message of man's divine state was also stated by Saint Paul in First Corinthians: 'Anyone united to the Lord becomes one spirit with him' (6:17), and in Ephesians: '...so that you may be filled with all the fullness of God' (3:19)."

Until now we have discussed the question of a symbiosis between two traditions, a spiritual "crossing over" brought about in one's own depths. At the heart of Swamiji there was still a more difficult gap to cross over. As he wrote to an old monk friend at Kergonan, "What interests me as the essential value of Hinduism is this—to find the Truth lying beyond the concept—not to remain [a] prisoner of concepts. Concepts are certainly valuable, but they are not absolute; they are linked to the evolution of human awareness. Therein lies the whole problem that upsets theology.... " And, I might add, upsets Swamiji in particular.

At this point, it is important to underline the fact that Swamiji experienced a true "Copernican revolution" in the field of interreligious encounter by wanting to become involved at a level beyond verbal dialogue, to live in his own heart and as a Christian the Upanishadic experience of non-duality. This is indeed the very heart of his saga.

In a letter to me he wrote, "I believe that it is necessary to go to the Hindu sources first of all in order to become capable of steeping oneself in the deepest Christian sources.... Non-dualism that is not experienced but merely thought is diabolical. It is one of those remedies which either gives life or it kills!" At the same time, he insisted that "the Truth of *advaita* does not destroy the truth at the level of interpersonal relations. The Truth of the Father and Son being face to face does not destroy the truth of their *advaita*: the Holy Spirit."

Odette, did Abhishiktananda ever share with you what went on in his heart and mind when he hid in the corn field while escaping from prison during World War II?

I cannot give any answer to this question for I never spoke about this with Swamiji. I can imagine that he did not take much time to think about what was happening in his heart but concentrated on acting without a second thought.

As a matter of fact, his regiment was encircled by the Germans who were proceeding to register their prisoners before sending them on to Germany. While queuing, he took advantage of a momentary absence of the sentry to run away and hide in the corn field until the regiment and the Germans had disappeared. Nearby, he was welcomed by a garage keeper who gave him a workman's overalls and loaned him a bicycle. He rode it home, where he remained in hiding for a time before rejoining his monastery.

All three "saints" of Shantivanam [Monchanin, Le Saux, Bede Griffiths] were intensely devoted to the Blessed Trinity. With Abhishiktananda it was, as you pointed out, a lifelong preoccupation. Could you talk a bit more about Le Saux's understanding of the Trinity, and especially about his description of "an explosion" that inevitably befalls anyone who experiences the Wisdom of Father, Son, and Holy Spirit?

If the "saints" of Shantivanam were so devoted to this Mystery, it was certainly under the pressure of the special circumstances in which they lived: the presence within two cultures—Hindu and Christian—of a Trinitarian notion of God, the Absolute: *Sat* (being) *Cit* (awareness) *Ananda* (bliss).

As regards Abhishiktananda, his way of theologizing was certainly influenced by his contact on the Christian side with the apophatic writers, especially Ruysbroeck, to whom he often refers. His way of thinking was more Greek than Latin. For him, the Father is the source of the Trinity.

But the Trinity was not a matter of speculation for Swamiji. It was rather one of personal experience. He writes, "I cannot understand anything of this Mystery if I have not felt—at least confusedly—in the most intimate depths of my own being the Mystery of being from Another and at the same time my non-duality with this Other." Perhaps his best formulation of the Trinitarian Mystery is this: "The Trinity is the face-to-face of the Father and of the Son in the non-duality of the Spirit. The Spirit is divine Love which opens Being up in a face-to-face relationship so that love can be expressed, and which closes it in *advaita* so that Love may be consummated."

Elsewhere we read: "Jesus appeared in the world not to teach ideas, but to share with humanity an experience, his own experience of being Son of God, and in the wake of this personal experience and by its power, to bring people to realize and integrate in their own awareness the mysterious dignity which is theirs also, that of being sons and daughters of God."

This experience of Jesus opens a path for us: "In revealing the secret of his Being, Jesus revealed the secret of every being. Everyone is charged with an essential secret, the Mystery of Triune Being." In other words, Jesus came to awaken us to our theandric dimension. To awaken signifies that we have to attain another level of consciousness, something that cannot occur without a *metanoia*, a conversion, an explosion, a turning inside-out of the whole being, a letting–go under the working of the Spirit. And Swamiji concludes, "The Father is the mystery of my origin and the Spirit the mystery of my relation to my Origin." Translating this in Upanishadic terms he explains: "The 'Further Shore' is only reached by the nuclear fission of the little self, by its violent breaking open at its greatest depth...." It was this inner explosion that he experienced at the time of the heart attack in July of 1973.

Reflecting on his experience he explained to Raimon Panikkar: "Really a door opened in heaven when I was lying in the street, but a heaven which was not different from earth, which was neither life nor death but simply Being, beyond all myths and symbols."

It is interesting to notice that Thomas Merton also felt such an explosion and described it as follows: "This realization at the apex is a coincidence of all opposites (as Nicholas of Cusa might say), a fusion of freedom and unfreedom, being and non-being, life and death, self and non-self, human beings and God. The spark is not so much a stable entity which one finds but an event, an explosion which happens as all opposites clash within oneself" (quoted by C. Nugent in *Cistercian Studies*).

Thus, we see that the three "saints," plus Thomas Merton, use the same word to signify the suspension of the mind's functioning on the level of duality, the ascent beyond names and forms to the Kingdom of the "Unnameable."

Can you describe briefly for us, Odette, what you call the "inner journey" or the "extraordinary spiritual journey" of Swamiji?

Swamiji's extraordinary spiritual journey cannot be dissociated from his daily life. His ordinary life is spiritually extraordinary! Please allow me to go back to Arunachala in 1952 at the time he was living in a cave as a Christian hermit amidst Hindu solitaries. It is in these grandiose and austere surroundings that the first great spiritual breakthrough took place. In his own words, "The realization of the all-pervading Presence of God in my actions, in my being, as in everything." The next year he confided to his diary, "The Christian *sannyasi* discovers with astonishment that in reaching the peak of Arunachala, he has penetrated into the very heart of Hinduism. He, Christian as he is, has realized the fundamental experience of Hinduism, the experience that one exists.... What is to be done? Only one thing. If the Christian Mystery is true it will appear intact on the other side of the non-dualistic experience.... Reason may discuss, but experience knows."

I want to stress that Swamiji remained until his last breath absolutely loyal to Christ. One may say that through his *advaitic* experience his Christian faith was not weakened but immeasurably deepened and purified. This has been precisely his charism.

In his book *Saccidananda* he expressed his experience in beautiful terms:

> In my own innermost center, in the most secret mirror of my heart, I tried to discover the image of him whose I am, of him who lives and reigns in the infinite space (*akasha*) of my heart. But the reflected image gradually grew faint, and soon it was swallowed up in the radiance of its Original. Step by step I descended into what seemed to me to be successive depths of my true self—my being, my awareness of being, and my joy in being. Finally nothing was left but He Himself, the only One infinitely alone: Being, Awareness and Bliss, *Saccidananda*. I had returned to my Source. "You are that!" were the last words I heard: "*Tat tvam asi*" as the Upanishad says.

Twenty years later he described this spiritual birth in terms of Light: "He who receives this dazzling light is transfixed and shattered. He can no longer speak. He can no longer think. He remains there beyond time and space. Alone within the solitude of the Self. It is a maddening experience, this sudden irruption of fire and light."

In December 1955, Le Saux was introduced to another Hindu sage, Sri Gnanananda. It was he who was to set the seal on Abhishiktananda's initiation to the spirituality of the Upanishads. During his stay with Gnanananda, Le Saux noted in his diary: "I cannot escape from the conviction that he is my guru, mysterious ways of Providence! In him I feel the truth of *advaita*. I should need months, perhaps years of profound silence to determine my position in this matter which transcends the intellect." Years later he wrote to me: "With Gnanananda I had a marvelous experience of the transmission from guru to disciple."

Toward the end of 1956, in order to integrate all that he had received from Ramana Maharshi, Mount Arunachala, and Sri Gnanananda, Le Saux undertook a long and austere retreat of thirty-two days, shut up in an underground room of a little temple. Besides his breviary, he took no book; his food was handed in through the window. Once the Eucharist was celebrated, his sole activity, apart from long hours of meditation by day and night, was writing in his diary.

The death of his companion Monchanin in 1957 marked a decisive step in Le Saux's life. The ashram monastery interested him less and less, for no Indian Christian ever came to join the two French priests. Now his thoughts were directed towards the Himalayas in order to live as a Christian among Hindu monks, who live there in great number. He walked and walked with the pilgrims to the sources of the Ganges, and he finally settled down in a very small hermitage in the heart of the Himalayas, while at the same time maintaining the ashram of Shantivanam in the South until he could hand it over to Father Bede Griffiths. By that time, his life was a *fait accompli,* one single faithfulness to two visions.

The year 1971 marked a new and most important stage in his inner evolution. Some genuine disciples came to him: two Hindus and Marc Chaduc, a young Frenchman. Swamiji discovered a new human dimension: spiritual paternity. In Marc he found a true and wholehearted disciple. All three, he said, "consider me as their guru and are for me a human relationship which reaches the most intimate depth of paternity. They take everything from me without depriving me of anything."

The fierce solitary lion is tamed by his own sons—his disciples! Marc was a seminarian with four years of philosophy and theology behind him. His own inner journey was not made of much pain and anguish. He came to India, met Swamiji with a list of questions, but the dialogue did not last more than a few days. There was no drama of conscience—another character, another generation, a different flexibility. There was a kind of spiritual osmosis flowing between the two. Afterward, Marc never had any doubt. His trust in Abhishiktananda's veracity was total, and his commitment absolute.

More frequently than in the past, Swamiji now left his Himalayan hermitage to devote his time to Marc, and in 1972 he went to sojourn in Phulchatti, a small ashram hidden in the jungle upstream from Rishikesh. They devoted the whole time to meditative study of the Upanishads. This study resulted, flowered, or rather exploded in both of them in a single experience. In a letter Le Saux wrote to me, he said: "Days of extraordinary fullness in Phulchatti—an intoxicating experience of the truth of the Upanishads, even if for me it was physically shattering. To feel oneself in the Presence of the True is too powerful an experience. It scorches one!"

After returning to his hermitage he suffered the first attack of breathlessness. This was never again to leave him, and when complicated by a heart attack, finally carried him off the following year.

In 1973, Marc recognized a deep call to monastic life, a call that he had heard almost from the very beginning of his encounter with Swamiji, and it found its realization in the *sannyasa diksha*—the monastic profession in an ecumenical form. This ritual ceremony was performed simultaneously by the Benedictine monk Father Le Saux and Swami Chidanandaji, the Hindu monk who was head of the well-known Shivananda Ashram in Rishikesh. Swamiji's last book, *The Further Shore*, was written in anticipation of this ceremony. In this way Marc, renamed Ajatananda, "gained admission to a twofold monastic inheritance, Christian and Hindu, in the unity of the Spirit." Two weeks later, on July 14, Abhishiktananda suffered the severe heart attack that laid him low in the street of Rishikesh and brought him his final Awakening.

At long last, the painful confrontation between his Christian faith and the Upanishadic experience had found its reconciliation beyond all possible formulations. East and West had found their meeting point, their one and unique source in the Spirit.

Finally, on December 7, 1973, the pilgrim of the Further Shore reached his goal, his whole being now harmonized, unified, at peace, radiating an inner bliss; entirely faithful to Christ his Sadguru and wholly immersed in the depths of his soul in his ground.

He could apply to himself what he wrote many years earlier of the Hindu sage: "A sage is one who has penetrated into his own source and recognized in the secret of his heart, the Self, the Mystery of God in His Epiphany."

You asked me to describe what I call extraordinary in Swamiji's spirituality. I think I have already quoted more than enough of his extraordinary statements. Nevertheless, let me conclude with one that I find typical of his daring spirit, always remembering that they were formulated thirty-four years ago: "O Lord, I had come to India to make you known to my Hindu brothers. And it is You who made yourself known to me through their mediation. Why did you hide yourself in this manner to give me your grace?"

The urge to discover for himself the truth of the Hindu inner experience must have been overwhelming to make him dare to embark on this adventure outside all existing Church regulations fifteen years before Vatican II. Last, but not least, what a tenacity he had to demonstrate to continue this enterprise against every obstacle, sustained only by his spiritual instinct and an intense inner dynamism, not to say a very special call of the Holy Spirit!

Odette, so often those of us who have lived some time in India say that the East sheds light on the Gospel. How did Abhishiktananda describe this in his experience?

Please remember Abhishiktananda's remarks when he first met living Hinduism: "The ashram of Ramana Maharshi helps me understand the Gospel; there is in the Gospel much more than Christian piety has so far discovered." His first discovery was the sense of the universal presence of God, which is at the heart of Indian spirituality. Hindu sages and pious Hindus, men and women, do not make any distinction between the sacred and profane; for them everything is holy and belongs to the Spirit's domain. This made him reflect more deeply on the words quoted by Saint Paul in his speech to the Athenians: "In Him we live and move and have our being." He stated that to pray is to realize that the Divine Mystery in its fullness is at once within us and without us, that it is totally immanent to our innermost being and at the same time infinitely transcends it.

A verse from the Taittirya Upanishad accompanied him all his life: "In this space that is within the heart, therein is the Person immortal and resplendent....That verily, from which all things are born, that by which when born they live, that into which when departing they enter. That, seek to know. That is Brahman—God, the Absolute" (5,9). Swamiji described that Hindu experience which he had shared since 1952 as follows: "At once so deeply Hindu and so deeply Christian, I contemplate the Reality, and the vision is painful; it is as if my two eyes were not adjusted. I need appropriate glasses to correct this. Once the sight adapts the vision will be marvelous." It will be "the real Baptism,....a new outlook on myself and on the world, not an intellectual knowledge, but an abysmal, cataclysmal transfiguration of one's being. Lightning. Thunder!"

Simultaneously, Swamiji clothed this discovery in Christian terms: "Man is renewed at the precise point at which he was created. For that, he has to descend to that level of his own being at which he is nothing but the image of God, to the place where, at the very Source of his being, nothing exists but God."

Swamiji was persuaded that, for Jesus, his Baptism had been the experience of his own source, the Father, but when Jesus discovered the Father, he did not discover an "Other"—"The Father and I are One!" He discovered his non-duality with the Father. In the Spirit he understood the voice that had been calling him "Son" and he answered: "Abba." To emphasize his understanding of this mystery, Abhishiktananda added, "The Baptism was perhaps the most important event in the life of Jesus. Easter only spelled out the Mystery. At Easter his going to the Father was outwardly manifested; but at the Jordan he realized that he was the very "I AM" of Yahweh."

Swamiji's oriental experience helped him the better to understand Christian love: "From the point of view of Jesus, my neighbor and God are not different. All live in communion that is both human and cosmic. The Last Judgment will not depend upon our acts of notional faith, but upon our recognition of the theandric Mystery that Jesus is in each human person: "I was hungry and you gave me food...." When was it that we saw you hungry and gave you food?.... "Just as you did it to one of the least of these who are members of my family, you did it to me" (Matthew 25:35,37,40). The divine Presence shines through my neighbor as truly as it shines in Jesus."

Another example: Looking at the wandering Indian *sannyasi*, Swamiji better understood the instructions which Jesus himself gave to his Apostles when he sent them out to preach the Kingdom. It involves nothing less than selling all that you have....Do not store up anything for tomorrow anymore than the birds. Leave behind your fields, house and family and take nothing for the road.... Eat whatever is set before you.

Finally, after his "extraordinary spiritual adventure," as he called the intense realization which occurred symbiotically at the moment of his heart attack, the best image he found to express it was a typical Christian symbol: "In this adventure I have found the Grail and the Grail is neither far nor near, it is beyond all places."

Let me conclude with a personal remark. This confrontation between an Indian spirituality and a Christian spirituality is, in a certain manner, the problem all Christians have to face today, each one according to his or her personal character. Out of my experience, I know how essential it is to face it adequately, that is, to be deeply rooted in one's own faith and spirituality. By spirituality I mean one's own total commitment to God and at the same time familiarity with our great mystics who have also approached God, the Ultimate Reality, through apophatism: mystics like Ruysbroeck, Eckhart, Suso, and, last but not least, our great women mystics of the Middle Ages—Beatrice of Nazareth, Hadewijch of Antwerp, Marguerite Porete, and so many others who walked symbiotically on nuptial mystical paths or that of the mysticism of Being. Chronologically speaking, they may belong to the thirteenth or fourteenth centuries, but in reality they belong to a certain "spiritual family" that has no historical boundaries. They help our intellectual approach to the Hindu scriptures, especially the Upanishads. This is a step that is, in my opinion, a must if we want to encounter our Hindu partner in depth at the level of the Spirit in the "cave of the heart."

Odette, you speak of Swamiji's charism and his spiritual path essentially consisting in the complete appropriation of the *advaitic* experience of the Upanishadic Rishis without losing hold of his rootedness in the Christian tradition. I sense you are more convinced of this than ever. Can you share with us your present conviction and some of the sources you draw from for this?

Good gracious! I wonder what words I could use to persuade you of my conviction of Henri Le Saux's total loyalty and faithfulness to Christ, the Church, and his Benedictine community. I believe that all my answers to your questions were pronounced against the background or backbone of this loyalty!

The first concrete source of my conviction is certainly the seventy-eight letters that he wrote to me during the seven years before we met face to face in India, and the profound spiritual friendship that blossomed through the years. Of course, I do not pretend to be infallible, but only to have an instinct like that of a hunting dog and to have been one of the very few who met Swamiji at a deeper level after his final finding of the Grail, and witnessed the wonderful peace, inner freedom, bliss that radiated from his whole being.

It was with a humble voice that he stated, "I can only testify to an experience—stammering it out—whoever possesses several mental or religious or spiritual languages is unable to absolutize any formulation whatever it be.... All my statements are only research vectors.... I don't want to theologize.... I leave it to the next generation."

Another source of my conviction is my deep connection with Marc, with whom I spent a fortnight in Europe while he was waiting for the renewal of his visa, and another two weeks in Rishikesh on the initiative of Swami Chidanandaji, in spite of the fact that he was already leading a solitary life.

What message do you feel Swami Abhishiktananda would give to people today, especially for monastic men and women interested in interreligious dialogue?

I think that Swami Abhishiktananda would shake with laughter and repeat: "Ah! It is always the same! People want ideas and never think that what they need first of all is to sit in silence and listen to the Spirit."

But then, with a very serious face, he would add, "I have only one message, the message that Jesus and all sages and saints of all traditions and of all times proclaim: The face-to-face with death, with God; the utter nakedness of this face-to-face. Death here means the 'Great Death,' not the physical one, but the disappearance of ego–centeredness." After this declaration he would certainly end his sentence with a wonderful smile and say: "It is so simple: open your eyes. Ah! the Awakening and the Quest is over!"

Swamiji was and is a voice crying in the desert, in the desert of humanity's mediocrity. But he is certainly not a model to imitate. With humor he used to say: "One clown is enough!" And again: "I do not want to leave some ideas to remember, but a new interior sense, an unformulated awareness of the Presence of God. The value of the words I was able to speak to you lay in their resonance rather than in their immediate meaning. Once conceptualized, this Truth which I bear is no longer true."

Maybe he would conclude with these words written in 1969 in his book *Hindu Christian Meeting Point:* "It is only in the depths of their own spiritual experience that Christians and Hindus alike are able to understand each other, and thereby outgrow the limitations inherent in every tradition. Only those who have experienced in themselves the Mystery of Being may understand India's spiritual quest.... For them religion is no longer a conventional pattern of thought and behavior received from a tradition, but a living experience of God in himself and in the whole universe, with the necessary commitments that flow from it."

2

EARLY GLIMPSES OF ABHISHIKTANANDA

Thérèse of Jesus ODC

Sister Thérèse of Jesus was a French Carmelite nun at the Carmel of Shembaganur.[1] She arrived in India shortly after Henri Le Saux. She later founded the Carmel of Soso in Bihar where Abhishiktananda was a spiritual director. This chapter first appeared in number 12 (June 1989) of the Occasional Bulletin *of the Abhishiktananda Society.*

I had the privilege of meeting Swamiji at a very early stage in his spiritual adventure. I had come to India two or three years after him, and we met for the first time in 1953, when I had been for two years in the Carmel at Shembaganur, a community of Indian Sisters near Kodaikkanal.

This is how we met. Two Little Sisters of the Sacred Heart of Father Charles de Foucauld were staying in our guest house while they were searching for a place of their own and learning Tamil. They had already met Father Le Saux at Shantivanam, and he had gladly agreed to give them some talks on Indian life and spirituality. So he came to Shembaganur and, as he was staying with the Jesuit Father nearby, he presented himself in his black habit. "You see me as a good Benedictine," he laughed. In those days, his normal dress was the orange garb of the *sannyasi*, but that was frowned upon by Christians. Things have changed a lot since then.

From the first, we met at a deep level. On his side, having a purely Benedictine background, he was delighted to be in contact with the contemplative life of Carmel, one lived in the spirit of pure *nada* (nothing) of Saint John of the Cross, which was my own inspiration and guiding line. This orientation was very close to the *neti, neti* of the Upanishads, which he was discovering at that very moment.

On my side, having been "parachuted" directly from a cloistered monastery in France into an even more strictly enclosed one in India, I had no opportunity to become acquainted with Hindu life and spirituality. But the Swami became for me a window on India, and by sharing his experience with me, he enabled me to discover many things and to taste the spiritual riches of India and my Hindu neighbors.

After that, our spiritual experience at the Hindu–Christian level was never to be separated, but rather merged in the pure Realization of the Self, from which there is no return. Though he has reached the Further Shore, I am still waiting—briefly, I hope—for the final wave to bring me to the other side.

For those who know Abhishiktananda only through his writings, or who met him only in his later years when he was well known and respected as "Swamiji," I will try to give a glimpse of what he was like at the beginning of his time in India. It will be interesting and encouraging to see how much he changed, or rather, developed, "unfolded"—for his life was a continuous pilgrimage of deepening discovery.

When I met him in 1953, his was still a youthful figure of medium height. His shaven head and the orange-colored robe of a *sannyasi* marked him out, whether he was moving among the Hindu villagers living beside the river Kavery or in Christian circles in Trichinopoly. No doubt his appearance could initially shock the pious in these circles, but people were drawn to him by his smiling affability. His simplicity and openness, his eagerness to discover spiritual truth, combined with a burning enthusiasm, sometimes led to exaggeration and lack of discretion, and people noted his tendency to get carried away. He suffered from a defect in his speech, which was made worse by his timidity. At times, it was very difficult to follow what he was saying (or rather, murmuring between his teeth), especially when he spoke a mixture of Tamil, Latin, Greek, French, and English! It is not surprising that many people thought him odd.

He had a strong sense of wonder and greeted every new discovery with enthusiasm. He was thrilled at the least glimpse of new spiritual experience. His previous Benedictine formation—rather rigid, and centered on the praise of God in liturgical worship, together with spiritual reading—had left little room for a deep personal experience of the Self within. In India, Father Le Saux discovered the interior prayer of the heart in the depths of his soul, going beyond all words and thoughts to reach the *guha*, that inner cave where the Self pervades all, and to find there the Realization of the Self at which Hindu spirituality aims through *dhyana* (meditation). His life in the contemplative ashram at Shantivanam and in the caves of Arunachala provided the setting for a real and deep experience of the Absolute. His reading and study of Hindu scriptures (Upanishads, Gita, Vedas) also pointed the way. His experience was therefore an interweaving of Hindu and Christian experience, each influencing the other, and so intricately connected that he was faced with the agonizing problem of finding a theological explanation for the presence within him of two such different religious experiences.

In those days, at the dawn of his spiritual development, the least hint, the least spark, of spiritual experience in another soul was for him an occasion for exultation. When he met someone on the way to Realization, or already diving into the depths of the *guha*, he at once responded, sharing his own experience. It was as if the Spirit was exulting in the depths of his being and that of the other.

I remember the day when he came up to Shembaganur to share with me his new discovery of the Fatherhood of God. He was still living in the South when this great event took place in his inner life, and God revealed to him the deep meaning of the Divine Paternity. His previous formation had been focused on Christ, but now, through his Hindu experience, Christ had led him to the Father. I can still hear him saying, as if in ecstasy, "Abba! Abba! Father!," emphasizing each syllable, "Ab-ba, Ab-ba, Fa-ther!" After he had several times repeated these words with jubilation, we were both (while standing on either side of the grill in the parlor) plunged into deep silence, a living silence full of the Presence of the Father. Abba! Abba! OM! OM!

There was, however, another side to all this. Like any youthful genius, dazzled by the discovery of the Self, the inner *guha*, he was astonished not to find the same experience in other religious and spiritual people. He expected everyone to live as if they too had had the same experience. At times, we sense this in his letters and other writings.

Like other prophets, he did not find recognition or acceptance during his early years at Shantivanam, apart from the few true friends who were moving in the same direction. He suffered deeply from being misunderstood, and his solitude made him all the more sensitive, vulnerable, and even touchy. Any criticism or unkind remark left a deep wound, and for some time afterward he would be very low and dejected. However, he would get over it and once again renew his efforts to find appreciation and approval, for at this stage he had not yet learned detachment from the opinion of others, which is the mark of a true *jnani*.

I recall that once, when he came to our Carmel, he discreetly offered to give a talk to the community, but our dear old prioress refused, afraid that the sisters would be shocked by his *sannyasi* robe. He had similar experiences on other occasions. For instance, when he appeared at the gate of a convent in Bombay, he was violently chased away by the porter, who shouted that it was no place for beggars and *sadhus*! And when eventually he met the superior and introduced himself as a priest and monk, she rushed to the phone to ask the bishop if he knew anything about this strange person! Later, of course, we could share a good laugh at these incidents.

During these early years, Father Le Saux was constantly hoping to find a *chela* (disciple) who would share his vision and enable Shantivanam to develop. Several times, he thought he had found the ideal disciple, but each time he realized that he had been mistaken, and hope turned into disillusionment. He had to wait until the end of his life for a true disciple to appear. This was Mark Chaduc, whose coming coincided with the last stage in Swamiji's enlightenment. At last, his dream of spiritual paternity was realized, at the same time as the final blossoming of his inner life before the departure for the further shore.

The fact that he was living much of the time on his own as he was having these new experiences and was, at the same time, so generally misunderstood, created in him an intense need to share his thoughts and experiences with those few friends who could understand and who themselves had a contemplative experience such as he himself was seeking.

From time to time, when he felt he must tell someone else about his experience and discoveries, he would come to Shembaganur. There, in the course of our conversations in the parlor, he would pour out at great length the thoughts that filled his heart to bursting. He knew that he could speak with full freedom, holding nothing back. In all simplicity he allowed his thoughts to flow freely and would perform mental somersaults without fear of being scolded or called to order at the theological level. I would mostly listen in silence, but I sometimes told him that these were spiritual acrobatics and that he was performing on a mental trapeze. Then he would come back to earth and burst into a roar of laughter. He well knew that this was all the Lord's *lila* (sport), and that he was still struggling in the depths of *maya* (illusion). We could laugh together, for he never took himself too seriously.

By nature he was a thinker, an intellectual. His mind was always active, on the move, though he strove to pass beyond the turmoil of thoughts to pure contemplation in the depth of the soul. There were moments when this was realized, as he noted for instance during his long silent retreat, and as I myself witnessed one evening long afterward, when he was with us in our new foundation of Soso at Bumla in Bihar.

In the afternoon we had had a long talk, and he had also spoken with all the sisters together. Then at five in the afternoon, when we withdrew for our customary hour of mental prayer, he went out to walk and pray beside the small stream that flows along the edge of our compound. The scenery in that lonely spot was tinted with crimson and orange in the fiery glow of the setting sun. The solitude and silence of the Carmel drew him into deeper contemplation beyond word or thought, and he experienced something like a "Taste of the Divine," a direct contact with the absolute, the *purnam* (fullness), which cannot be described.

That evening we had planned that he should lead us in singing *bhajans* during our time of recreation, but when he returned from his walk, he took me aside and begged to be excused, as it was impossible for him to speak. After receiving such a grace, he had to remain alone in silence. When I gave my consent, he smiled, and the light in his eyes told far more than any words that could have passed his lips. So we parted with "OM."

The most striking impression that I retain from those early years of contact with Swamiji is that his life was one of constant movement between solitude and the world. As the ocean waves ebb and flow on the seashore, so he would often retire to one of his hermitages to taste the Divine, to plunge into the *guha*, the Abyss of the Self. But he could not remain there for long, and he would soon return to establish human contact. It was not his calling to be a solitary hermit, and he had to come back to the shore of this life, to put his experience to the test, to share them with others, letting them also draw from the gushing waters of the same Source.

This is surely something that can inspire our life, whatever may be our situation in this world. We cannot live as a hermit, a *sadhu*, a *guhantara* (dweller in the cave), but we can always keep alive in the depth of our being a thirst for the shore that is "within." We can always find time to withdraw for periods of solitude and silence, immersed in the Ocean of the Self, and then return to the shore of this world, refreshed by the water of divine life. To enter into the cave of the heart—even if it can only be for a short while, for a few minutes, in the midst of a busy life in this world—will always enrich us, and will be a source of enlightenment for others. The contact with the Divine will become deeper and deeper as we advance on the road towards the *purnam*, the fullness. So we may share with Swamiji a glimpse of the radiant light of the all-pervading Self.

OM! *Purnam*! OM!

3

PILGRIM AND HERMIT

Bettina Bäumer

Dr. Bettina Bäumer is an Austrian Indologist who has lived and worked in Varanasi since 1967. She was President of the Abhishiktananda Society from 1988 till 2007. She was also Director of Research, Alice Boner Foundation; Hon. Consultant, Indira Gandhi National Centre for the Arts; and Visiting Professor in Vienna University. Her main fields of research within Hinduism are Kashmir Shaivism, the temple architecture and religious traditions of Orissa, and comparative mysticism. This chapter first appeared in number 72 (May 2004) of the Bulletin *of the North American Commission of Monastic Interreligious Dialogue.*

It is precisely the fact of being a bridge that makes this uncomfortable situation worthwhile. The world, at every level, needs such bridges. The danger of this life as a "bridge" is that we run the risk of not belonging to either side; whereas, however harrowing it may be, our duty is to belong wholly to both sides. This is only possible in the mystery of God.—Swami Abhishiktananda, Letter dated September 2, 1967.[1]

This passage sums up the vocation of the French Benedictine monk who immersed himself in the spiritual world of Hinduism to become as fully and completely as possible a Hindu *sannyasi.* In this process, Swami Abhishiktananda did not take lightly the demands of asceticism and discipline of both traditions, nor the theological implications of this "belonging wholly to both sides." It was a struggle and a complete surrender to this very special call "in the mystery of God" that made it possible for him finally to attain the goal and to reach equilibrium. By treading this difficult path he has opened a way for others—not only for Christians in their meeting with Hinduism, but for persons seeking a spiritual meeting between any two spiritual traditions.

I can never forget my first meeting with Abhishiktananda. In Rome, Raimon Panikkar had given me Abhishiktananda's first book, *Hermits of Saccidananda* (in French), which ignited me. I was then a student, twenty-three years old, and I was irresistibly drawn to meet this hermit in the jungle of South India. Thanks to Panikkar, this first journey to India became possible, and in November 1963 I visited Abhishiktananda in his Shantivanam Ashram. The inner contact was immediate and I could feel his deep involvement with India, her people, her spirituality, and especially with *advaita* as lived by Sri Ramana Maharshi. Abhishiktananda's enthusiasm was contagious. I was equally impressed by the utter simplicity of his life, a quality that would stay with him till the end of his life. Although deeply in love with silence, he had an urge to communicate with kindred souls. He spoke with me about his meetings with spiritual personalities. I was very inexperienced at that time, with little knowledge about India, but he never gave me any feeling of inferiority. Rather, he had the gift of drawing out the best of a person and lifting her up to his own level.

I would like to stress some points that were especially characteristic of Abhishiktananda but do not emerge very clearly from his books: his great simplicity of life and his indomitable faith in the spirit of India. In spite of being misunderstood—more often by his Christian brethren, but also by others—he was never discouraged from following the path he had chosen, and he never lost faith. In fact, there were not many who could understand him, and he passed through phases of loneliness—not a psychological lack of company, but the price he had to pay for the uniqueness of his path. As he wrote in his diary on November 18, 1970: "The hermit must accept the Solitude of God. If he tries to fill up this solitude with gods or with the supreme God, he does not obtain the Supreme Abode.... [I should] accept the indescribable solitude of God, not manifested, without a name, without sign, and not fill my solitude with the thought of this solitude."[2]

Another sign of his true contemplative spirit was his love for nature—in Shantivanam it was the majestic river Kavery that inspired him, and later, in the North, the sacred and wild Ganga (the River Ganges) flowing by his cottage in Uttarkashi.

Many years later, when I settled down in Varanasi in 1967 and was working with Raimon Panikkar, Swamiji used to come for a visit, sometimes using this as a stopover on the way from the South to the Himalayas, and these were always times of intense discussions and spiritual sharing with Panikkar, myself, and a few friends. Swamiji would also celebrate some unforgettable liturgies in the Indian way of worship in the small chapel of the Little Sisters of Jesus by the Ganga or at the students' chapel. The word "experimental" is not fitting for those liturgies; they were rather his natural way of integrating the beautiful symbolism of the Hindu *puja* [ritual] with his "attachment" to the Christian tradition, letting them flow together and giving each its own place and significance. The transformation that took place within him at the crossroads of two completely different traditions always found expression in his liturgical celebrations, until it reached the utter simplicity and almost wordless form of the last months of his life. The Mass never ceased to have meaning for him, but it was a meaning that was neither static nor repetitive—it was always a new discovery. So we find this entry in his diary: "The Mass is not for getting anything whatever—nor is communion, for I have everything from the moment I exist—but it is like the expression of my being, like the expectation of and approach of the moment that comes in the moment that now is, in the same way as I draw breath in the power of this actual moment, bringing about also my presence to the moment which is coming" (December 1, 1970).

Another aspect of the human side of Abhishiktananda that is known only by those who had met him personally was his sense of humor. It somehow belonged to his down-to-earth character and his natural humility. He could laugh at himself and did not take himself too seriously. Unlike some spiritual persons, he did not mix up the seriousness of his concerns and ideals with his own person. Without compromising his ideals, he accepted the contingency of the human condition. And therefore, when ultimately the supreme experience overwhelmed him, it was only the Divine, the Ultimate Reality, shining through him, reflected in his "eyes of Light."[3]

Thirty years have now passed since the time of this great experience and his passing beyond[4] (how much he loved this word "beyond," *au-delà!*) to the "further shore of darkness" (cf. Svetasvatara Upanishad). What, then, is the relevance of the life and thought of this hermit in our contemporary situation of interreligious dialogue?[5] Both India and Christian theology have changed tremendously in the last thirty years. Was not his ideal of a spiritual India too idealistic? And was not his Catholic theology based too much on the historical form it had in the forties and fifties of the twentieth century? Yet in spite of these changes (to which he would certainly have responded had he lived a few decades more), the message of his life and thought is still not only relevant but even prophetic.

Religion and spirituality play an increasingly important role in our times, but they are often distorted, either by a narrow fundamentalism or by a superficial esotericism and eclecticism. The interreligious dialogue taking place in air-conditioned five-star hotels among religious leaders and intellectuals—necessary as it may be—cannot really penetrate to the core of the problems of a multicultural, multi-religious world, divided into rich and poor nations. Swami Abhishiktananda experienced in his own person the encounter and tension between two different worlds—East and West, Hindu and Christian (in over-simplified terms)—and taking both seriously he attained new insights and an integration at the spiritual level. His discoveries—based on sometimes painful, but more often blissful experiences—have far-reaching implications: for the Church, for a new spirituality, for a true inter-religious understanding. By giving a call to go "beyond" names, forms, dogmas, and institutions he did not mean a cheap escapism from the spiritual or theological demands of one's tradition, but he showed a way of transformation, in the light of a deep encounter. It is not possible within the limits of this essay to work out the implications of such a meeting, as elaborated by Abhishiktananda himself and as they could be developed on the basis of his insights and applied to new situations, both in India and in the West. But it can certainly be affirmed that Abhishiktananda's most important contribution in this field was an authentic mystical experience at the confluence of two traditions.

4

IN SEARCH OF LIBERATION

George Gispert-Sauch SJ

*Father George Gispert-Sauch is a Spanish Jesuit who has
lived and worked in India since 1949. He presently teaches
at Vidyajyoti, College of Theology, Delhi. This chapter first
appeared in number 20 (November 1999) of* SETU, *the Bulletin
of the Abhishiktananda Society, and consists of extracts of a
talk he gave at a book discussion on March 29, 1999, at India
International Centre, New Delhi, to mark the appearance of
the English translation of Swami Abhishiktananda's diary,*
Ascent to the Depth of the Heart.

I have long admired Swami Abhishiktananda, even if I met him
only three or four times. One could speak at length and humor-
ously about the lively Breton who would burst into song in the
middle of the chores of dish-washing and could hold an audience
fascinated by the glow of an inner vision that was conveyed more
by his eyes than by his clumsy words. He was a monk nostalgi-
cally humming the Gregorian cadences of his early youth in the
same breath as he submitted all structure, mental or ecclesiastical,
to pitiless criticism. He could as much laugh at himself as poke
fun at others, and yet his message was always about the Absolute
Brahman and our search for liberation. One could speak in contra-
dictions of the absent-mindedness of an intellectual that he did not
like being and the practical sense inherited from his Celtic fisherman ancestors. But since it is futile and impossible to transmit a

personal experience, I will just trace the high points of his rather simple yet extremely rich life, because they form the background to the evolution of his thinking.

Dom Le Saux wanted to come to India not only to continue his personal search for God in a less structured religious culture, but also to give to the monastic life—particularly the Benedictine tradition—of the Church a new *avatara* in India, a new expression that would enrich it. This could only be done through a humble presence and a dialogue in depth between the Hindu and the Western tradition.

This, today, we call inculturation, a word that has become current in Christian theology only in the last thirty years or so. Abhishiktananda's diary is a personal testimony of this process. Both his diary and his abundant correspondence give us a fascinating glimpse of the process through which God was training this monk, and of the results of that process.

Abhishiktananda discovered that the Indian spiritual tradition required from him a total stripping of his mental apparatus, of his theological and over-rational approach to God, and of the strongly activist element of the spiritual *élan* developed in the West. He did not have to strive after God, but to discover God within, by removing all the mental layers that seemed to prevent the eternal light from shining. There were moments in his encounter when he seemed to be at the point of renouncing his Christian faith in favor of a Hindu wisdom. The fascination of his diary is precisely in seeing that he never lets go of two commitments. He is certain of both views. "The Upanishads are true. I know it," he exclaims toward the end of his career on earth, and yet he never lets go of his Christian moorings. In the last page of the diary he speaks of Christ as the one who has lived the Trinitarian Mystery discovered in the depth of the Self. His celebration of the Eucharist continues to the end of his life, if he was physically able. He does feel a tension, even a contradiction, within himself, but he is sustained by a higher force not to let go of either expression of Absoluteness.

The power of Abhishiktananda's writing is that he refuses easy solutions of the problem of the meeting of the two great religions that sustain him in his monastic search. He will not make of Christianity a mere *sadhana* (spiritual practice) at the *bhakti* (devotional) level that needs to be left behind at a higher level of *gnosis*. But he equally refuses to see Hinduism as a "preparation for the Gospel" (*preparatio evangelica*), to use the old expression of Eusebius so often repeated in Catholic theological circles. From within the Hindu tradition he perceives that this understanding is not possible. The two visions, though irreconcilable as far as our mental perceptions are concerned, must be held as absolute and valid.

The experience of life forced Abhishiktananda to redefine his own identity. He had come to India in search of God, surely, but not merely as an individual seeker. Christian monk that he was, he always saw that search in a communitarian perspective. His vocation, his call, was to bring to the Church in India the value and dimension of contemplative life and to live it in an Indian way, grafted into the old traditions of Hinduism, and indeed of the even older tradition of the Sramanas. He hoped that this vocation would be realized by a group having a certain continuity. But his vision of an Indian Benedictine institution proved a mirage. His hope of communicating his personal experience and witness to at least some disciples seemed futile, at least till almost the end of his life. He would be a solitary voice that would bear witness but not be heard. His role would end with his life. He then saw that the contemplative life is really a life that does not properly belong to any religion. Religion deals with structures and the world of signs. The contemplative deals with the invisible world. He or she is a paradox, a sign beyond all signs. In this sense Abhishiktananda believed in a brotherhood/sisterhood of all contemplatives of all religions, whose main purpose is to relativize all forms of worship, all theological concepts, all the world of *namarupa* (name and form), all religion, therefore, in function of the One.

Was he unconscious of the social obligations of our earthly existence? Was he unaware of the enormous problems of our world, where millions starve while enormous wealth is accumulated and concentrated in privileged regions of the earth and in privileged homes of every region? Was he sensitive to the social problem? He was. He did a fair amount of sharing of the little he possessed. He knew of the sin of the world. But he believed that it could only be redeemed with deeper consciousness of the Absolute Reality. He believed that the absence of God was much more terrible than the absence of bread, because it cuts at the very root of our humanity. Some of us may think that this his option was warped. That may be the difference between us and the mystics.

5

GOD'S HARP STRING

Vincent Shigeto Oshida OP

Father Vincent Shigeto Oshida (1922–2003) was a Japanese Dominican who created a small community at Takamori, a village in the Japanese Alps. The members of his community live in solidarity with their neighbors and practice a way of life made up of manual labor, prolonged Zen meditation, open personal communication, and Christian liturgy. This chapter first appeared in number 16 (December 1982) of the Occasional Bulletin *of the Abhishiktananda Society.*

There was some secret within Dom Le Saux that he revealed to no one, a certain vision in the secret place of his heart that was so much "him" that he did not disclose it in any way, not even perhaps to himself. "Even the wickedest, even the meanest, is not excluded from Christ"—not precisely this, but something like this, not a concept, however, but a living Light that suffused the natural light of his intelligence and enabled him to choose instinctively the more essential.

The uniformity of his life—a hermit's life constantly maintained in spite of his outgoing tendencies—discloses the existence of a Secret within him. His single-eyed devotion to his own *raison d'être* is not to be attributed to some "Breton" quality of flint-like persistence.

When Jean Leclercq, the French medievalist, came to our fraternity, So-an, situated in the mountainous part of Japan, I took him to see our nearby spring, and before leaving he presented me with a copy of *Une messe aux sources du Gange* (*The Mountain of the Lord*) by Dom Le Saux. Ever afterward, the freshness of our gushing spring reminded me vividly of those "sources of the Ganges" described by this unknown and yet somehow intimate person.

In the same year, 1968, at an international conference on monasticism held in Bangkok, I heard that Le Saux had been one of the invitees, but that he had declined to come. This fact turned my attention to him more seriously.

In 1970, I received a visit at So-an from Murray Rogers, who had come to Japan from India in connection with the East Asia Christian Conference. He urged and well-nigh compelled me to attend some of his meetings, and I discovered the spiritual solitude in which he so often found himself at these sessions. I could not forget the urgency of his face as we said goodbye on the platform of the station at Atami. Thus, when I received his letter of invitation to India, I could not find it in my heart to refuse. He was himself shortly to leave India. He told me that Dom Le Saux, whom I shall henceforward more properly call Swami Abhishiktananda or simply Swamiji, would also be waiting for me, having come down from his hermitage at Uttarkashi in the Himalayas. I knew of the close relationship that existed between Swamiji and Murray. I sensed in this letter something bigger than friendship. I felt that something very symbolic was taking place.

Jyotiniketan, the small community of which Murray was the leader, was an indispensable place for Swamiji in the carrying out of his vocation. Here was one of the few places where he could feel himself really at home and understood—somewhere where he could talk freely and unburden himself of some of the mental suffering inevitable in one whose blood, despite his manner of life, was still inexorably French.

Together, we made the pilgrimage to Hardwar and there, on the first night as we sat on the bank of the Ganges, Murray put the question: "What has Christianity meant to this land of India?" I said a few words and then fell silent, and we continued to sit in a deep quietness under a crescent moon, listening to the rapid stream. I was "listening in" to the one Mysterious Note that was and is at the source of the integrity of both my companions, a note sounded by the principal string of the harp of God on which he has lovingly played since the world began.

Four years later, Murray and I were together in the Old City of Jerusalem. It was there that we received the news of Swamiji's death. I remarked to Murray: "There are certain others endeavoring to live a Christian community life in India in the Hindu style, but it seems to me that the atmosphere of their lives is a little different from that of Swamiji. Don't you think so?" He replied: "I think it is very different. He dived simply and completely into the Ocean of Hinduism." This man who once before, when taken prisoner by the Germans, had after an hour and a half clambered through a hedge and jumped from there to freedom, plunged later into the Ocean of Hinduism, this time to remain for the rest of his life. And this time he leapt in naked, retaining nothing. You would know what I mean if you watched him, dressed as a Hindu swami, enter a shop on a narrow street to buy a little napkin of cotton or some other small item that forms an indispensable adjunct to the Indian way of life.

But I must tell you of another harp string, lest I be guilty of a grave omission. The harp string that I just referred to is the harp string of Soul and Spirit. Now I will speak of the harp string of Body and Heart.

I perceived in Swamiji a remarkable thing. Despite the completeness of his dive, his own character and nature, even his Western education, remained "safe and sound" within him, without loss or diminution. Herein lay the drama of his soul.

Swamiji lived among Hindu *sadhus* and swamis in a natural manner, and even became an Indian citizen. For him, this was simple and straightforward; and yet, at the same time, he remained simply and equally himself. This deep dive into Hinduism had inevitably meant a complete rupture with the past. In his daily life his past remained hidden, unknown to those among whom he moved. For some twenty years, he was cut off, physically at least, from his fatherland, his family, friends, and Benedictine confreres, and from the culture that shaped him from his birth through his early years. Never again did he taste the bread, cheese, and wines of his childhood. He never returned to France.

During the first week of my stay in Jyotiniketan I was confined to my bed, and each day, morning and evening, Swamiji came to visit me—and long were our talks if Murray, fearful lest I be over-tired, did not come to take him away! Sometimes during these talks, Swamiji would allow to escape his lips those inner thoughts that will never be published. On one such evening, all the members of the ashram gathered in my room for recreation and evening prayer, and I suggested to Swamiji that he should sing us a song of Brittany. He covered his face with his hand in a quick movement and after an intake of breath stayed very still, instinctively doing violence to some inner urge. He did not weep, but I saw the trembling of his heart within him. The silence was heavy, and I regretted my own thoughtless stupidity. After a few moments he started to sing a Breton fisherman's song in a rather broken voice. It was only then that I realized the intensity of his drama.

As we walked round the streets of Hardwar, Swamiji spoke of his own Thomistic training and the Gregorian chant that figured so prominently in the Benedictine life. Then, while walking on the banks of the Ganges, he told me of something that had happened in a Hindu ashram in Lucknow a few years earlier. Swamiji was in the ashram kitchen and was watching two girls, both Catholics, who were making chapattis. It was Christmas time. One of the girls began to sing a Gregorian chant piece from Christmas, and the other soon joined in. They, like me at Jyotiniketan, were quite unaware of the drama of Swamiji. Suddenly, the repression of many years gave way, and he cried out explosively, "Stop, please stop!" "It was," he said, "an *ecartelement,* a real *ecartelement* (being torn asunder)." An older Hindu who was standing by said, "Christ is here. I am looking at him."

This second harp string is intertwined with the first so that, like soul and body, they cannot be distinguished.

God played on this harp a melody that was little known but very beautiful, and one of the most beautiful notes of all was, I think, the last—so clear, so transparent, though rather solitary: solitary, and yet a culmination and summary of all the rest. The last touch of the hand of God sounds often the most exquisite note of all. He fell in a street of Rishikesh, stricken by a heart attack. Some months later, never fully recovered, he entered the sleep of deep peace in the Sisters' hospital at Indore.

Oh, praised be God by that beautiful harp that was Swamiji himself! We await the day when we shall hear your music once again and now transfigured. May you receive the reward of your solitude.

Surely the beauty of his music will one day be revealed—the music of this man whom many regarded as a weird and even crazy monk.

PART TWO

The Meaning
of Abhishiktananda's
Experience for Spirituality
and Theology

6

Abhishiktananda and the Challenge of Hindu–Christian Experience

Bettina Bäumer

This chapter first appeared in number 64 (May 2000) of the Bulletin *of the North American Commission of Monastic Interreligious Dialogue.*

There are several reasons for taking Swami Abhishiktananda as a model for the "challenge of Hindu–Christian experience." For one thing, Abhishiktananda understood from the beginning of his encounter with Hindu spirituality that it is not a question of entering into dialogue with "another," but that there is an inner challenge within Christianity, which is in need of the spiritualities of Asia in order to overcome the deep crisis of Western Christianity.

In the development of Abhishiktananda's life, experience, and thought, we can discover a process with different stages—from the convinced missionary with a certain fulfillment theology to the stage of one who was shaken by a real encounter with Hindu spirituality and torn apart by two experiences, two "ultimates," two identities, two worlds of religious expression, and, in his own words, "two loves." From there, he passed to a third stage, that of relativizing all formulations, all "names-and-forms," all concretizations of the one, unspeakable, inexpressible Mystery. Finally, he came to a stage of re-identifying the "correspondences," which he discovered at both ends of his experience in the light of an "explosion" of all previous concepts. With all his theologizing tendency, Abhishiktananda remained aware of the dangers of re-naming or re-defining the Reality that is beyond all names and forms. He could not completely escape this danger, but the reflections expressed in his spiritual diary, which he often pushed to the extreme, are very helpful for those who have come after him and are trying to trace the stages of this process.

To the end, Abhishiktananda remained faithful to his two identities—his belief in Jesus Christ and his acceptance of the Hindu experience of *advaita*—whatever may have been the final synthesis that he discovered. I would like to stress the following points in the experience of Abhishiktananda as being of utmost importance for our approach to the future of Christianity and the future of religion in general in the twenty-first century:

1. One cannot (or should not) throw overboard one's own religious/cultural/spiritual roots when encountering another religion. Even those post-Christians who think that they have no roots cannot deny some hidden identity that has to be integrated in one way or another.

2. At the same time, one has to take the other tradition as seriously as one's own.

3. The dialogue of religions is not a device, not only a way to understand the other, not just an academic exercise or an institutional duty, and certainly not an esoteric trip. Rather, it is the only way to respond to the challenges humanity is facing at this turn to the twenty-first century, within and without. At the same time, it is a way to rediscover our own identity and to relativize our false certainties.

4. Such a dialogue has to take place at the spiritual level, rather than at the conceptual/academic or the social/institutional levels. The latter are also necessary, but they have to follow. This implies a stripping, an emptying of our cherished beliefs and concepts, a plunge into the depth of the Divine Reality without any support. This may not and cannot be the task

of everyone, but just as in other human fields there are a few who perform a certain task for the whole of humanity, so also in this field.

Abhishiktananda used to insist that one should not try to imitate him. His way was unique and yet has a pioneering value for all of us. At his time, the very idea of "double belonging" would have amounted to heresy, but it has now become an almost accepted term. Perfect *advaiti* that he was, he might have made his own the strong words of the Katha Upanishad: "Whoever sees diversity/difference here, only goes from death to death" (4.10–11). And yet he was not for facile reconciliations and compromises. Indeed, this is a path "on a razor's edge," as the same Katha points out (3.14).

ABHISHIKTANANDA'S EXPERIENCE

We may look at Swami Abhishiktananda's experience as paradigmatic in the context of the four stages of his discovery as we find them documented in his spiritual diary.[1] As Raimon Panikkar writes in the Introduction:

These pages offer a fascinating example of the evolution of a thought-process. They enable us to witness the coming to birth of a conviction, the fruit not of theory but of practice. The intellectual experiments with his ideas, the monk does so with his life. Life itself, and not reflection, is the source of his thoughts and convictions, which are born from and develop out of his lived experience....

The value of the private diary of this monk lies neither in the ideas that it contains (they are expressed better in his books), nor in the evidence of a life (this would better emerge in a biography), but in its revelation of the depths of a human being, in his subconscious levels. We witness the development of a soul's archetypes under the influence of two different cultures. To live at the meeting point of several traditions is the

destiny of a large portion of the human race. For very many
people it is hardly possible any longer to feel at home in a single
culture. To camp out in the workshops of technology does not
answer to human aspirations. A new insight is required. This is
where Abhishiktananda's experience seems to me to be of great
importance (pp. xv–xvi).

We need not stop very long at the first phase of Abhishiktananda's
conviction, which was very close to that of Abbé Monchanin: the
fulfillment phase. As an example, we can point to his exclamation
when celebrating the first Christmas in India in 1948: "The mystery of Christmas, great here! Respond in the name of my people
to the Father's call! As Jesus came to respond in the name of the
world to the Father's call to the world.... Be the summit through
which my people reaches God" (December 19, 1948, p. 2–3).

His meeting with Sri Ramana Maharshi in 1948 soon shook
his fulfillment theology. In the light of this perfect incarnation of the *advaitic* experience, all the deeply entrenched convictions of Christian superiority seemed to crumble—though
Abhishiktananda was always able to distinguish between Christ
and his followers (a distinction that brought forth more anguish,
since he was also a lover of the Church). The Christian fulfillment
idea was rather turned around: it was in the heights of Hindu spirituality that he found his expectations fulfilled.

The tensions created by the meeting of Hindu spirituality at its
highest and purest level were partly theological, partly psychological and spiritual. A theology of the absoluteness of Christianity
that is centuries-old cannot easily be overcome. But the real challenge for Abhishiktananda was in the psychological and spiritual
realm, where he had to ask himself whether he was up to the mark
of such a perfect state of consciousness as he encountered in Sri
Ramana Maharshi and later in Sri Gnanananda. This challenge
remained with him till the end of his life:

What gnaws away at my body as well as my mind is this: after having found in *advaita* a peace and a bliss never experienced before, to live with the dread that perhaps, that most probably, all that my latent Christianity suggests to me is nonetheless true, and that therefore *advaita* must be sacrificed to it.... In committing myself totally to *advaita*, if Christianity is true, I risk committing myself to a false path for eternity. All my customary explanations of hell and the rest are powerless against a reality that exists in a way unknown to me.... Supposing in *advaita* I was only finding myself and not God? And yet, it is only since I made the personal discovery of *advaita* at Arunachala that I have recovered peace and a zest for life.

What guru will enlighten me?

I pray as a Christian, but I am well aware that all those words are external. The only truth is *quietas* at its actual source, within. The *guru* comes at the moment when you are ready, says Hindu wisdom. What is the *guru*, ultimately, but the outward projection of this thirst for the Self?....(September 25, 1953).

Being caught in this dilemma, he evidently tried to solve it at all levels, including that of reflection, as for example when he compares the beyond-death experience of Saint Paul and of Ramana:

Paul had the experience (*anubhava*) of Jesus alive, although previously Jesus "had died," the experience of a dead man who had come back to life, and to a definitive life that "can never be taken away," by means of a faith in which henceforth everyone could himself attain to life opposed at the same time to death and to evil, for death and evil (sin) went together in Hebrew thought.

Ramana had the experience (*anubhava*) of "self-being," not of a dead man come back to life, but of a "so-called" mortal who possessed being in his inmost depths, in the only true way, that which senses that this being "can never be taken away," by any power whatever, whether of nature or of will (December 10, 1959).

The creative and painful tension between the two experiences would stay with Abhishiktananda until the end of his life, where it got dissolved at a higher level. But creative it was and remains for us, because only when one takes both traditions seriously can there be tension. And Abhishiktananda took the traditions seriously, not only in their peak experience, but also with the whole burden of their cultural, religious, historical, and philosophical differences. It was not an easy relativization, not a simple denial of the one in favor of the other. In fact, Abhishiktananda did not deny anything of what he previously believed; but everything was elevated to a level where the "names and forms" became insignificant.

The stage of relativization came, therefore, once he penetrated more deeply into the *advaitic* experience.

> Christianity and *advaita*: Neither opposition nor incompatibility—two different levels. *Advaita* is not something that conflicts with anything else at all. It is not a philosophy—but an existential experience. The whole formulation of Christianity is valid in its own order, the order of manifestation (*vyavaharika*) (and so, provisional), and not of the Absolute (*paramarthika*). The Christian *darshana* (worldview) is no doubt opposed to the Vedantin *darshana*, but this is merely the doctrinal level. No formulation, not even that of *advaita*, can claim to be *paramartha* (October 23, 1970).

The solution to the anguish and tension cannot be found at the conceptual level: "And people would like to have conceptual solutions—ready-made formulas like those that come out of a computer—for their problem: Christianity/Vedanta. The solution lies only in the original anguish of the person" (September 7, 1970). As he wrote a year and a half later:

> Concepts are dualistic and therefore falsify everything that they claim to express about what is beyond *dvandvas* (pairs of opposites). The *dvandva*: man/God in Jesus to start

with; the *dvandva*: sin/virtue, salvation/damnation. When Naciketas asks Yama what is beyond religious law and irreligion (*dharma/adharma*), beyond made and not made (*krita/akrita*), etc., Yama simply answers with OM! Truth cannot be formulated, at least at the luminous apex where all its splendour is concentrated. It can only be *abhiklipta*, integrated, experienced, received (*upalabdha*)—in the sense that the mind is wholly "passive." No role for the intellect as agent. No mental framework for one's reading (April 2, 1972).

We have seen in Abhishiktananda's own words his first fulfillment phase, the second phase of crisis while encountering Hindu spirituality, and the third phase of relativizing all conceptualization and particularizations. What is fascinating is that there is a moment of "explosion," of "awakening," in his own cherished words, but an explosion which amounts to a liberation that did not destroy his faith in Jesus but transformed it.

Whether I like it or not, I am deeply attached to Christ Jesus and therefore to the *koinonia* of the Church. It is in him that the "mystery" has been revealed to me ever since my awakening to myself and to the world. It is in his *image*, his *symbol*, that I know God and that I know myself and the world of human beings. Since I awoke here [in India] to new depths in myself (depths of the Self, of the *Atman*), this symbol was marvelously developed.

Moreover I recognize this mystery, which I have always adored under the symbol of Christ, in the myths of Narayana, Prajapati, Shiva, Purusha, Krishna, Rama, etc. The same mystery. But for me, Jesus is my *sadguru*. It is in him that God has appeared to me; it is in his mirror that I have recognized myself, in adoring him, loving him, consecrating myself to him. Jesus not the founder-head of a religion; that came later.

Jesus is the *guru* who announces the mystery (July 22, 1971).

The ultimate experience that helped him to overcome the duality of his Hindu and Christian experience is in both traditions the final and true "I," *aham*.

> If God is that Being to whom nothing is either earlier or superior—as the Bible says (or even later or inferior, as the Upanishad says)—then he is in this very *I am* in which I awaken to myself. And it is not satisfactory to say that he is the "cause," the substratum. No, nothing can escape this *parama*, this Supreme Being. This *I am*, this awakening to myself, is the very awakening of God to himself (paradoxical use here of the third person). This awakening is at once within time and outside time. It is the awakening to a level that is in no way measurable by time.
>
> It is in this word *aham* heard in the depth of myself that the whole world was made, exists, subsists: the five elements, time, the human senses, the human body, etc....(all in view of this awakening. All a means to the awakening, all an ascent towards the awakening). This *aham asmi* (I AM) is the light of everything (*phos, jyothi*), the life of everything (*vita, bios, prana*). Beyond all darkness, *tamasah parastat*.
>
> This I AM (*aham asmi*) was made flesh (*sarx egeneto*).
>
> Christ is the total transparency of this *aham asmi* to which I awaken at the source of my consciousness. Christ—if he has any value for me—is the very mystery of this awakening to myself.
>
> He is the one who is totally awakened, even in his body (*deha-jagarita*) (*deha* includes the *manas*). Christ is the "symbol" *par excellence* of this awakening—but here are also Krishna, Rama, Shiva, Buddha....
>
> Christ is the revelation of my *aham*, of my mutual relationship (*paraspara*) with every consciousness, every awakening. Each person is the absolute, singular and unique, and everywhere each one is relative to the other. Each person comes from the other, each person is born of the other (July 2, 1971).

For Abhishiktananda, it was certainly not a question of finding a fascinating esoteric Hindu spirituality at the expense of the

Christian mystery. In the late stage of his experience he no longer sought theoretical solutions, but instead discovered wonderful correspondences, "upanishads," between the two spiritual experiences, precisely because he could see them from within:

> In the depth of the inner cave (*guha*) there is no name and equally no non-name, neither Shiva nor Jesus....
>
> Jesus is that mystery that "grounds" me, that "sources" me, in the abyss, in the bottomless *guha*—the mystery (as we say) of the Father—and *extends me*, pours me out (*expendit*) into all that is. The Spirit, the *prana*, who makes me the Self within everything (*antaratman, sarvantaratman*)—spread out into everything, lost just as truly in this expansion that infinitely multiplies me as agent, as in this "source-action," that infinitely reduces me, to be ultimately identical to zero....
>
> A being lost in my source, a being lost in my fulfillment. And in this very loss, I am.... Jesus is this mystery of *advaita* in which I can no longer recognize myself *separately*. Lost as much in the space (*akasa*) of the heart as in that of the span of the universe, as much in the Source as in the shining, the radiance that empties me.
>
> And I am Fullness, *purnam*; precisely in this letting-go of myself everywhere, *sarvatra*....
>
> And my *purnam* is precisely this emptiness of all self. The *kenosis* of Christ! (December 24, 1971).

At this stage there is *advaita* between his Hindu and his Christian experience, a true liberation from the bondages of traditions and concepts. There is a complementarity in the different approaches to the Absolute.

The very last entry in Abhishiktananda's diary makes clear how his "awakening" has made him transcend all the tensions that he had to go through in the earlier stages:

> The Awakening at the level of anyone who has consciousness is precisely to lose oneself, to forget oneself. The Awakening

is the shining out of the splendor—in splendor—of the non-awakening, of the eternal not-born. The non-Awakening, the not-born, is manifested by a—what?—a brilliance, a light, a glory that envelopes everything, that transcends everything, that seizes one and takes one beyond everything, a sense of "*Beyond*," of the Beyond....

The gift of wisdom, a deep connaturality, an explosion which one who has "felt" cannot evade....(September 12, 1973).

SHIVA AND CHRIST

The publication of Abhishiktananda's diary in English comes twenty-five years after he attained *samadhi*. To some theologians his ideas still seem to be too daring, too revolutionary, while others consider his theological problems outdated. At the existential level, some of the Indian Christians have tried to follow his ideal, with the danger of creating new *namarupa* (names and forms), as Abhishiktananda had feared. Others find his obsession with *sannyasa* one-sided and prefer a Dalit liberation theology. And yet, the liberating and explosive message of his life and experience remains very much valid and necessary. The only condition for making it fruitful is the utmost sincerity and transparency that was his.

What have we done in these twenty-five years since his passing? I do not want to give a history and speak about others who have trod a similar path. But I may dare to say something about my own experience of thirty-two years in a Hindu context. It is not my intention to be too personal, but I remember the reply of a Hindu friend when I had given a slide show about my pilgrimage to the most sacred mountain Kailash, and after that told him that I did not want to speak about my personal experience. He said simply: "What is personal? It is all universal." Allow me, then, to extract the more universal aspects of my personal experience.

First of all, not all those who tread a similar path have to pass through the same anguish that Abhishiktananda went through in his experience of two traditions. He has cleared the way for others. Second, though I was inspired by his example and encouraged by him since the beginning of my contact with spiritual India in 1963, I had to find my own way. Though the Upanishads and Ramana Maharshi were and still are fundamental in my plunge into Indian spirituality, it was the mystical tradition of Kashmir Shaivism that brought me the fullness I was longing for. This is not the place to give an introduction to this spirituality and philosophy which, in a way, is the culmination of Indian thought and mysticism. I can only mention the essential complementary aspects to the spirituality of *advaita* that was Abhishiktananda's main partner in dialogue.

In Kashmir Shaivism, as in *advaita*, we find a non-duality between the self and God, but in a theistic context. There is a personal relationship with God, Shiva, who bestows grace on the soul in order to make it recognize its true, original, that is, divine nature. The underlying philosophy is therefore called the school of recognition (*pratyabhijna*). Another important difference from the spirituality of Vedanta is the positive value of the body in spiritual practice and experience. Because of its Tantric background, the spirituality of Kashmir Shaivism is more incarnated than the acosmic *sannyasa* that was Abhishiktananda's ideal. The cosmos and the body are very much part of the process of liberation—the ideal being liberation during one's lifetime (*jivanmukti*). This spirituality is thus more sacramental, since all the acts of daily life are considered to be sacred and means for spiritual realization.

This is only a brief description of some of the concrete ways the spirituality of Kashmir Shaivism complements Vedantic spirituality. It is impossible to describe its philosophical depths and mystical heights. which lead to a state of perfect spontaneity, of Divine consciousness, where ultimately even spiritual practice is to be given up. To quote only one verse of Abhinavagupta's "Hymn to the Absolute or Unsurpassable":

What words can describe the Unsurpassable? In the Absolute can there be any distinction between the worship, the one who worships and the object of worship? How and in whom can there be spiritual progress? What are the degrees of absorption? Illusion itself is ultimately the same as non-dual Consciousness, all being the pure nature of the Self, experienced by oneself—so have no vain anxiety!

The conception of the Divine is so universal that the names Shiva, Bhairava, or others are never understood in any limiting, sectarian sense. That is why Utpaladeva, the great mystic of the early tenth century, can exclaim:

Glory to you, O Shiva, who are the essence of the "right handed" path, who are the essence of the "left handed" path [two opposing Tantric schools], who belong to every tradition and to no tradition at all. May you be glorified, O God, who can be worshipped in any manner, in any place, in whatever form at all (*Shivastotravali* 2.19–20).

But obviously, the reasons for being attracted by a spiritual tradition are not merely theoretical. It is a living tradition in its fullness that attracts and challenges. And the only response possible, as was the response of Abhishiktananda to Ramana Maharshi and Sri Gnanananda, is a total acceptance, respect, and, finally, surrender.

To observe a spiritual tradition from outside, to read its texts, is not sufficient if one wants to enter deeply. One has to accept it, in theory and practice. In the case of most Indian traditions, this also implies initiation. For me it was the meeting with Swami Lakshman Joo of Kashmir and being accepted by him in this tradition that opened the door to this spiritual world.

What happens then to one's Christian roots and convictions? There is an entirely inner process of encountering, absorbing, and letting the two traditions lead an internal dialogue without too much interference of the mind. It all happens at the level of pure consciousness, where the names "Shiva," or "Christ," are not important, but the reality lived and experienced behind those names. In any authentic experience, nothing can be lost.

We know that most Westerners who accept a spiritual tradition such as Buddhism or who embrace Hindu forms have been disappointed by Christianity and have thrown overboard their Christian faith. Another form of dialogue is required, different from that with the authentic representatives of the original traditions. Both are necessary, because we are more and more confronted with a kind of secondary tradition. But I am convinced that the discovery of the original living traditions is most essential for our Christian understanding and dialogue. It is pioneers like Abhishiktananda, who have experienced the other tradition from within, who are the best mediators, because they have undergone a process of transformation—a personal spiritual process that has wide repercussions.

CONCLUSION

The Hindu–Christian experience can have many consequences and conclusions, and it can lead to a fresh understanding of Christ The name Jesus Christ is heavily loaded by two thousand years of history and, according to Panikkar, "perhaps we should change that name because of the historical connotations of the last two thousand years.... Yet, it is in and through Jesus that a Christian experiences that mystery which Christians call Christ" ("Indian Theology and the Third Millennium").Whether or not we change the name, what is important is to rediscover the experience of "that mystery," and here the meeting in depth with Hindu and Buddhist spirituality can give an essential impulse. This also because the West has been culturally and religiously emptied and de-sacralized and it is very difficult to recover what has been lost. However,

I do not mean that these spiritual traditions should be used by Christians for resolving their crisis. This would be another kind of colonialism, where we exploit not the natural riches of another culture, but its spiritual riches. One has to be aware of this danger.

This meeting still remains a challenge, and we should have the humility of disciples learning and receiving, the intellectual honesty to accept the differences, and the deep respect for these traditions in their own right. But with these precautions, the meeting with Hindu spirituality can open a wide horizon, and it can also help us rediscover our own Christ. I shall mention a few points and concepts.

Abhishiktananda had developed the correspondences with the Vedic-Upanishadic *purusha*, the cosmic and inner Person, the Divine presence within:

> The *mythos* of the Purusha is wider than that of Christos; not only does it include the cosmic and metacosmic aspect of the mystery, but it is also free from attachment to time entailed by the *mythos* of Christ. Rather, it recognizes all the symbolic value contained in the mystery of Time, but refuses to compress the absolute separately into a particular point of time (February 17, 1973).

Jesus could also be described as the perfect *jivanmukta*, the one "liberated while living," the greatest ideal of Hindu spirituality, especially of its *advaitic* or non-dualistic forms. The *jivamukta* incorporates the divine perfection in his or her very body, by being transparent to the Spirit, the Atman. Sri Ramana Maharshi and Swami Lakshman Joo were perfect examples in the lifetime of Swami Abhishiktananda and mine.

Another important spiritual and theological approach to Christ is the guru, the *sadguru* or true master. Contrary to the misunderstanding and misuses of the importance of the guru in the West, in the Indian tradition he is the personal face of the transcendent

Reality, he is the visible form of the Ultimate: *guruh saksat para-brahman, as* every Hindu recites almost daily: *tasmai srigurave namah*, "to that Master be adoration." The guru is only recognized as such if he is transparent to the Divine Reality. The great mystic Kabir therefore expressed what most Hindus feel: that if he were to meet his guru and God at the same time, he would fall at the feet of his guru first, because it is through him that he has seen and experienced God. What could be more close to a Christology where Christ is the visible form of the invisible Father and the Master?

While Abhishiktananda would prefer that we speak of *Christ consciousness* rather than *Christology*, he would at the same time caution us to be careful that it remain at the level of a living experience and not become another concept! In Hinduism we find a variety of living spiritual traditions, but all are embedded in tradition. Hindus are aware that ultimately they have to go beyond all traditions once they have come to the realization of the Self, of God.

Abhishiktananda, who had carried the burden of tradition and at the end liberated himself from that same burden, would have surely rejoiced at the following verse from the Yoga *Vasistha*, a highly mystical text of *advaita*:

> The sacred scriptures are a burden for one who has no discrimination,
> knowledge is a burden for one who is attached,
> the mind is a burden for one who has no peace,
> and the body itself is a burden if one has not realized the Self.

7

ABHISHIKTANANDA AND SRI GNANANANDA

Nityananda Giri

*Swami Nityananda Giri is a noted spiritual teacher and scholar
of Vedanta. This chapter first appeared in number 64 (May
2000) of the* Bulletin *of the North American Commission of
Monastic Interreligious Dialogue.*

Sri Gnanananda, that great Himalayan sage and yogi who
made a very deep impression on Swami Abhishiktananda, was
a monument of a man, a legend in his own lifetime. He had conquered the aging process of his body and kept all people guessing
about his age. He would parry all questions about it, as many were
curious to know the secret of his longevity. He would exhort them
to inquire about the immortal Spirit within and not about the mortal perishable body, its vehicle. Nor would he speak about his *sadhana*, spiritual attainments, which were obviously extraordinary.
He considered that all achievements belong to the realm of the
ego. Nor would he talk about the disciples who would have come
to him in the past years for his guidance. He lived from moment to
moment, in the eternal now, with no thoughts of a dead yesterday
and unborn tomorrow.

Hence Sri Gnanananda's early life is shrouded in mystery. But
in all lives of great men, what is there on the surface to see? It is
believed that he was born in the early years of the nineteenth century in a village near Mangalore on the west coast of South India.
Even as a boy, he experienced a descent of grace (*saktinipata*), which

took him to Pandharpur, a great center of Maharashtra mysticism. There he met his guru, the pontiff of the northern regional center of *advaita* at Badrinath, established by the great philosopher saint Sri Sankaracharya. He had come to South India on pilgrimage. Sri Gnanananda accompanied his guru to Srinagar in Kashmir and after the latter's *mahasamadhi* (passing from this life) he spent many years performing austerities in the higher altitudes of the Himalayas. He visited Kailash in Tibet, Nepal, Burma, and Sri Lanka before he came to Tamil Nadu. The earliest we hear of him in South India is around 1860 near Chidambaram.

In the course of his wanderings on foot over many decades as a *parivrajaka* (itinerant monk) he had come into contact with the spiritual luminaries of the last century and the present one. Around the turn of the century he was staying in the Sampathgiri Hills of Polur near Tiruvannamalai. He was with Sri Aurobindo after his arrival at Pondicherry from Chandarnagore. Sri Gnanananda also recalled his meeting with Sri Ramana Maharshi in the Virupaksha Cave.

The swami was first and foremost a *paramahamsa parivrajaka*, a true wandering monk without belongings or obligations. He exemplified in himself that spontaneous love of insecurity and anonymity that is the hallmark of a genuine *sannyasi*. He moved away as disciples built ashrams for him. It was only toward the end of his phenomenally long spiritual ministry that he settled down at Thapovanam on the outskirts of the ancient temple town of Tirukoyilur on the banks of a sacred river and within the spiritual aura of Arunachala. The ashram is situated about a kilometer away from the four-hundred-year-old *samadhi* tomb of another great Hindu saint, Sri Raghottama Swami. It is located on the Tiruvannamalai-Tirukoyilur highway, about two hundred kilometers from Chennai.

The earliest residents of the ashram that grew around the sage's presence were monks, mainly from Sri Shivananda Ashram of Rishikesh in the Himalayas. Later, householders working in schools and offices nearby, as well as retired householders, settled down in the ashram to serve the swami. In this way, a great many persons, including women and children, were exposed to the influence of an ashram life. *Brahmacharis* came for spiritual guidance and had ample scope for service of the guru and the study of scripture under monks who trained them. There were also retired householders who came for initiation into monastic life.

Sri Gnanananda was deeply interested in monastic revival and gave initiation into traditional *sannyasa* to a few of those who had a genuine calling and were well prepared with the disciplines of asceticism and interiorization. The renunciate disciples were all given facilities for the study of Vedanta and the pursuit of a contemplative life. In 1969, Sadguru Gnanananda established a retreat center for them at Yercaud, a hill station, and called it Sri Gnanananda Pranava Nilayam. The name indicates that it is a center for meditation on Atman, symbolized by the *ardhamatra* or half-nasal ending of "OM," the *pranava*. There is no ritual or communal worship at Yercaud. The pictures of Sri Gnanananda, Sri Buddha, Swami Vivekananda, the Sacred Heart of Jesus, and the Kaaba at Mecca adorn the walls of the central hall.

Sri Gnanananda underlined the importance of Karma Yoga and Bhakti Yoga and held the traditional view that only one who has attained purity of heart, single-minded concentration, and a good degree of "desirelessness" by cultivating intense devotion to God is qualified for intense study of Vedanta and self-inquiry. In order to meet the needs of the largest group who came to him, he constructed and consecrated an ashram temple with various deities. Thus we find at Thapovanam *sannyasis* engaged in study and practicing meditation side by side with *bhaktas*, devotees singing *kirtans* in praise of the Lord. There are others who prefer ritualistic worship with Vedic chants. Thus the unique institution represents the many facets of the Master's personality.

It was at Thapovanam in December 1955 that Swami Abhishiktananda met Sri Gnanananda. He was already acquainted with the teachings of Bhagavan Sri Ramana Maharshi, the Sage of Arunachala, and of the Upanishads, and was attracted to the caves of Arunachala at Tiruvannamalai. Sri Gnanananda advised him to come again to Thapovanam in February 1956 for two weeks of retreat in silence and meditation. In his book *Guru and Disciple*, Abhishiktananda describes his encounter with the Master. He speaks of the retreat with him as "Days of Grace, days of peace and fullness, when one knows one exists in the depth of oneself where all appearances are left behind and one is on the level of the True." Sri M. P. Pandit of Sri Aurobindo Ashram writes, "I personally consider the book *Guru and Disciple* to be one of the major spiritual documents of the present century, far, far superior to many books from the West that have appeared of late."

Swami Abhishiktananda gives a vivid and moving account of his first meeting with Sri Gnanananda, whom he recognized as his guru, and reflects on the mystery of the guru. The guru, he says, is one who has himself first attained the Real and who knows from personal experience the way that leads there. He is capable of initiating the disciple and of making well up from within the heart of his disciple the immediate, ineffable experience that is his own— the utterly transparent knowledge, so limpid and pure, that quite simply "he is." When the vibrations of the master's voice reach the disciple's ear and the master's eyes look deep into his, then from the very depths of his being, from the newly discovered cave of his heart, thoughts well up which reveal him to himself. When all is said and done, the true guru is he who, without the help of words, can enable the attentive soul to hear the "Thou Art That," *Tat-Tvam-Asi*, of the Vedic Rishis.

Abhishiktananda goes on to speak about *guru darshana* with great feeling. Meeting in depth is *darshana. Darshana* is, etymologically speaking, vision. It is coming face to face with the Real. In a way, this is possible for us, in spite of our human frailty. There are philosophical *darshanas*, the systems of the thinkers which aim at making contact with the Real in the form of ideas. There is also the *darshana* of the sacred places or *kshetra*, of the temples and holy images or *murti*, where the Divinity who transcends all forms is willing to don the numerous forms invented by man's imagination when set on fire by faith. Above all, there is the *darshana* of holy men, the most meaningful of all for the man who is on the right wavelength. The *darshana* of the guru is the last step on the path to the ultimate *darshana*, when the final veil is lifted and all duality is transcended.

Abhishiktananda noted that Sri Gnanananda refused all cheap spirituality. He taught the way of total renunciation so that finally there is no ego left to manifest itself. His teachings are the same as that of the Upanishads. Behind the appearance of the veil of the empirical and phenomenal ego is the Ultimate Reality, which could also be called the Immortal Self of All, which is the same as God in the absolute transcendence as Godhead. The Ultimate cannot be an object of knowledge or experience. One has to be It, and that is the only way of knowing It. Being is Knowing. So, the Knower of Brahman, the Godhead, is the Brahman Itself, proclaim the scriptures. The external guru, the guru with the form, is *gurumurti*, who, having realized Atman, the Self, shows the way. He makes the disciple take the high dive and reveals his true form as the inner guru, the Atman, "I AM," who is *akhanda*, undivided, and *advaitic*, non-dual. Again and again, Gnanananda tells Abhishiktananda that *guru darshana* is the direct and immediate realization of Atman, the Self, "I AM."

When one attains this state of unitive consciousness, of being one with the Self of All, the *sarvatmabhava*, he truly becomes an embodiment of Infinite Love. Swami Abhishiktananda described

Sri Gnanananda by saying that his whole being radiated a pure and tender love, a love that was complete for each one and the same for all. The joy of being loved by him exclusively filled everyone and resulted in a high degree of detachment, for who does not dream of being loved apart from others and with a preferential love? Yet at the same time, each one experienced being enveloped in a plentitude of love. One felt that with Gnanananda all distinctions, *bheda*, had been overcome and had vanished. It was the personality of the Self alone, the Atman, in each person that was immediately perceived by him.

Sri M. P. Pandit, a great disciple of Sri Aurobindo and the Mother, said that Sri Gnanananda had infinite compassion, a compassion born of strength, *Atmabala*, strength of Bliss. In one of the most ancient Upanishads, there is a description of the one who has realized the Divine Self. He is *Atmakrida*, one who sports with the Self; *Atmamithunah*, one who has the Self for his companion; *Atmananda*, one whose delight is in the Self. Whenever he looks at a child, a plant, a flower, or an animal, he sees only the Self. He lives and joys in the Self, *Atmaratih*. Sri Gnanananda is such a one who has stepped out of the pages of the Upanishads.

Sri Gnanananda received devotees of all ages, of all stages in life, of all races, men, women, and children. He reminded them again and again that human birth is rare to obtain, and that the goal of life is God-experience, that is, Self-realization. A Jesuit priest from Tamil Nadu who was drawn to *advaita* was advised by Swami Abhishiktananda to meet Sri Gnanananda. He asked the sage whether he should become a Hindu to pursue his *advaitic* Vedantic *sadhana*. Sri Gnanananda told him that there was no need to change his religion. Vedanta is the transcendent element in all great religions. He should go deep into his own religion and discover it there. *Advaita* would make a Christian a true Christian. Later, the priest became an internationally known teacher of Zen meditation.

Sri Gnanananda often emphasized that one should graduate from the religious life to the interior and contemplative life so that he might realize God as his own Self, which is the transcendent element in all religions. This seems to have made a deep impression on Swami Abhishiktananda. In his brilliant and inspired essays on *sannyasa*, he wrote that every religion is for its followers the supreme vehicle of the claims of the Absolute. However, behind the *namarupa*, the names and forms, behind external features such as creed, rites, etc., by which it is recognized and through which it is transmitted, it bears within itself an urgent call to pass beyond itself inasmuch as its essence is to be only the sign of the Absolute. In fact, whatever the excellence of any religion, it remains inevitably at the level of the signs and it remains on this side of the Real, not only in its structure and institutional forms, but also in its attempts to formulate the inevitable Reality in mythical and conceptual images. The mystery to which it points overflows its limits in every direction. Like the nucleus of the atom, the innermost core of any religion explodes when the abyss of human consciousness is pierced to its depth by the ray of pure awakening. Indeed, its true greatness lies precisely in its potentiality to lead beyond itself.

CHRIST AND COSMIC CONSCIOUSNESS

Following this short account of Sri Gnanananda's life and teachings, I would like to offer, from the perspective of Vedanta, some reflections on Christ and on cosmic consciousness, and also to refer to the Christ experience of Swami Abhishiktananda, the disciple of Sadguru Gnanananda.

I should confess at the outset that I have not studied Christian theology or Christology or even the Bible in full and in depth. But I have been blessed and enabled by the grace of Sadguru to look at Christ through the eyes of the great Christian mystics, like Saint Teresa of Avila, Saint John of the Cross, Thomas à Kempis, Meister

Eckhart, and others. As a keen student of mysticism, and with the background of Vedanta, pronouncements like "You should lose Christ to find him" appear to me to be of very special significance.

It is spirituality that India seeks in its religious quest, and not a creed or dogma. With its genius for mysticism, its passion for the direct and immediate experience of the Divine and consequent spiritual hospitality, the Indian mind recognizes in the Lord Jesus Christ an Avatar, a descent of the Divine in human form. Great Hindu sages like Sri Aurobindo and Sri Ramakrishna have hailed Jesus Christ as an incarnation of God. His advent, like the extraordinary birth of an Avatar described in Hindu scriptures, was an event heralding universal joy. The Bible describes how a group of shepherds received in the stillness of the night, in an extraordinary way, the intimation of the birth of the Lord: The shepherds were amazed. Hardly had they time to recover from this amazement, when they heard a multitude of angels singing and praising God: "Glory to God in the highest heaven, and on earth peace among those whom he favors!" (Luke 2:14).

The Avatara is a dual form of divinity and humanity. The Divine takes upon himself a human nature with its limitations and creates the circumstances, means, and instruments for transcending human nature and realizing the true divine nature. Hence the Avatara tries to conceal his true nature as God. Yet the divinity in him sometimes peeps out spontaneously. We can see this in the Gospel, as when Christ tells the woman, "Thy sins are forgiven" (Luke 7:48), or in his words of promise, "Come to me, all you that are weary and are carrying heavy burdens, and I will give you rest" (Matthew 11:28).

When one has developed the highest devotion to God, the Lord lights up the lamp of wisdom in his heart and reveals his true nature to him. How? First as God, as the Lord of the creation, who creates the world out of himself, out of his free will, and moves about in it, without being bound by it, just like a spider that weaves a web out of itself and moves in it freely. He is *Visvanatha*, the Lord of the universe. He is imminent in creation. Creation itself is the form of God, *Visvarupa* or *Visvamaya* . However, he transcends creation; he is not exhausted by creation since he is infinite. He is *Visvadhika* (beyond the universe). This is God in relation to the creation. He is the cause.

Is this vision of God complete? No, it is not. He now reveals himself as the ultimate reality too, which transcends cause and effect, which is beyond creation or even before creation was thought of. What was there then? Only God by himself and nothing else. It was all one God, the relationless absolute. It is then not called God, as this word always implies creation. This transcausal one is called by Meister Eckhart *Godhead*. Vedanta calls it *Brahman*. God and Godhead are to be understood as two states of the One Reality: the Relative and the Absolute, the Becoming and the Being. The Godhead is the *plenum* of undifferentiated existence beyond time, space, and causation, which is called *sat*. This existence is also awareness by itself. This self-awareness is the core of all knowledge of things constituting multiplicity, and so it is called *cit*. Because of the infinitude of the existence which is awareness, it is bliss, *ananda*. It is not joy, for that is only a changing state of the mind. This infinite *ananda* includes and transcends all joys known to earthly and celestial beings.

Now we have to examine the relationship of the embodied soul to this God or Godhead. This is the unique mysticism of the Upanishads, which the scriptures assert to be a matter of universal intuition. Christian mystics like Meister Eckhart bear witness to it. The infinite that is the Godhead is the innermost core of the embodied soul as "I AM" Awareness. By analyzing the three states of consciousness that encompass the whole experience of man, namely, the waking, the dream, and the deep sleep states, one will arrive at their unchanging witness as "I AM." It is *sat cit ananda* as experienced in the state of deep sleep itself. The subject–object relationship is seen to be in the relative state only. That the subject and object coalesce in *nirvikalpa samadhi* is the meditative experience of the mystics. Therefore, the innermost core or essence of God is the same as the infinite, immortal self, *atman*, which is the core of the embodied soul. This is what Jesus proclaims when he says, "My Father and I are One."

We see something similar in the following words of Meister Eckhart:

> When I came out of the multiplicity, then all things proclaimed: "There is a God" [the personal creator]. Now this cannot make me blessed, for hereby I realize myself as a creature. But in breaking through, I am more than all creatures, I am neither God nor creature. I am that which I was and still remain forevermore. There I received a thrust that carries me above all angels. By this thrust I am so rich that God is not sufficient for me, insofar as he is only God in his divine works. For in thus breaking through, I perceive what God and I are in common. There I am what I was. There I neither increase nor decrease. For there, I am the immovable which moves all things. Here man has won again what he is eternally and shall ever be. Here God is received in the soul.

With the grace of God and the highest spiritual disciplines of meditation and self-inquiry, one overcomes completely his false identification with the body, mind, intellect, and ego. Then he discovers his true being as *atman*, which is *sat cit ananda*. It is the same as Godhead or Brahman, which is God without being qualified by the manifesting power. That is why Eckhart calls it "barren Godhead." When one has the self-realization as "I AM," he is in the non-dual awareness of *atman-brahman*. He has realized his oneness with *brahman*, which is the essence of God. One who is established in the "I AM" awareness has realized his true nature to be infinite and has crossed all sorrow and delusion. He is called *jivanmukta*, a person liberated while alive. In turn, as a compassionate *sadguru*, a *guru* one with all existence, he gives the saving knowledge of the reality to all. He is a savior. Vedantic texts describe the state of his consciousness, qualities, and behavior. It is with this purpose that we may imitate him by developing those same qualities and attitudes and ultimately have our ego consciousness transfigured into the divine consciousness, when one sees God everywhere. Jesus Christ is such a *jivanmukta* and a savior. His pronouncements, such as "My Father and I are one" and "Before Abraham was, I am," speak of the state of his consciousness. His compassion and infinite love can be seen in him as the Good Shepherd. He is the *sadguru* who delivers the Sermon on the Mount.

ABHISHIKTANANDA'S CHRIST EXPERIENCE

Swami Abhishiktananda's life was marked by an intense inner conflict between his Christian upbringing and training as a theist and the powerful attraction of the *advaitic* acosmism of the Upanishads. It took time for him to experience the fact that the acosmism of *advaita* is based on a very sound theistic foundation. The inner conflict ended with the experiences he had just before and after his heart attack of July 14, 1973. Even earlier, his zeal for the mystic quest, his burning desire for salvation, could be seen in his letter to a friend who had visited the Holy Land. Referring to Christ as a *sadguru*, he writes:

> You meditated at the place where the "*Sadguru*" lived, meditated, prayed, and taught.... But did you discover his presence? As an archaeologist, you live so naturally in the past, but the past is dead. You must surely, some time or other, have enjoyed those words of Angelus Silesius, "What good does it do to me that Christ was born, died, and rose again so long as that is not true in me?" India effectively frees us from the whole past,

as from the whole future. There is only the Eternal moment in which I AM. This name (I AM) which Jesus applies to himself in Saint John is for me the key to the mystery. And it is the discovery of the Name in the depth of my own "I AM" that is truly Salvation for each of us.

In a letter to another friend on the anniversary of his baptism, he writes: "My wish for you is that the 'Awakening' which began on that day may lead you more and more to the discovery of this 'I AM' in which alone you will meet the Christ, no longer in a memory or in beautiful, theological ideas, but in his mystery, which YOU ARE yourself."

When we read Swami Abhishiktananda's description of his experience of "I AM," it is clear that he left far behind all his theological attempts to get the *advaitic* experience into a Trinitarian framework. He says, "Who can bear the glory of transfiguration, of man's dying as transfigured; because what Christ is I AM! One can only speak of it after being awakened from the dead.... It was a remarkable spiritual experience." Or again: "The only thing that counts is that I myself am, and that has nothing to do with time. I AM with the eternity of God, since I am born of God. The theologians are afraid of the assertions of the Gospel and I had to go by the way of Hindu scriptures in order to accept the Gospel paradoxes in their full truth."

After the spiritual experience, Abhishiktananda declined an invitation to a Muslim gathering in France to give the Christian point of view. He wrote about this to Murray Rogers:

The more I go (on), the less able I would be to present Christ in a way which could still be considered as Christian.... For Christ is at best an idea, which comes to me from outside. Even more, after my "beyond life/death experience" of 14th July [1973] I can only aim at awakening people to what "they are." Anything about God or the Word in any religion which is not based on the deep "I" experience is bound to be simply "notion," not existential. Yet I am interested in no Christology at all. I have so little interest in a Word of God which will awaken man within history.... The word of God comes from/to my own "present," it is that very awakening which is my Self-awareness. What I discover above all in Christ is his "I AM." It is this I AM experience which really matters. Christ is the very mystery that "I AM," and with the experience and existential knowledge all Christology has disintegrated.

The Gospel of the Christ is the Gospel of spiritual redemption. It is the discovery of the Christ as He is, the Eternal Christ, the "suchness" (*tathata*) of the Christ in terms of the Gospel as "I AM." Only then will oft-made statements such as "The Christ must be born in you" or "It is in dying that we are born to Eternal Life" become meaningful; only then will the perennial philosophy in the teaching of the Christ become a lived truth; only then will a direct and immediate mystic experience of "AHAM" carry its own certitude.

OM TAT SAT

8

Enveloped by Mystery

James Wiseman OSB

Father James Wiseman is a Benedictine monk of Saint Anselm's Abbey in Washington DC, professor of theology at the Catholic University of America, and long-time member of the Board of Directors of Monastic Interreligious Dialogue. This chapter first appeared in number 45 (October 1992) of the Bulletin *of the North American Commission of Monastic Interreligious Dialogue.*

In the final months of his life the great twentieth-century German theologian Karl Rahner was one day asked about an article he had written more than thirty years earlier entitled "Forgotten Truths concerning the Sacrament of Penance." Rather than talk about the article, he answered with a dark mien and sad tone of voice: "It's anything but a matter of some forgotten truths or the forgetting of a sacrament! Nowadays even God is denied, as well as the frightful reality of sin."[1]

Two years before that exchange, he had published an article on the Church and atheism in which he claimed that the struggle against atheism is above all "a struggle against the inadequacy of our own theism" and then suggested that Christians try to form an alliance with the followers of other theistic traditions in order "to learn something from one another for their respective faith in God" and to enable pastors better to preach "on how people today in all seriousness can have a living faith in God."[2]

A superficial interpretation of that recommendation might lead one to infer that these various theistic traditions all have clear and distinct concepts of God, which can then be amalgamated in some ingenious way to produce the desired pastoral effect. Rahner himself would, of course, have disavowed any such interpretation. From his earliest writings, such as the long essay on "The Concept of Mystery in Catholic Theology,"[3] to his numerous later reflections on the need to develop a mystagogy of Christian faith, he not only dwelt on the reality of God as absolute Mystery but also regretted the fact that for most theologians "the incomprehensibility of God is the content of an individual thesis about God" but "does not from the very outset always and everywhere permeate our understanding of God."[4]

What would it be like if this "thesis" did truly permeate a person's understanding of God? And would familiarity with such a person's thought significantly correct what Rahner called "the inadequacy of our own theism"?

One way of approaching these not insignificant questions is to examine the spiritual journey of a man, Henri Le Saux, who did come to feel utterly and thoroughly enveloped by the incomprehensible mystery of God. Up to the present time, his thought, when familiar at all to contemporaries, has usually been gleaned from two books that he published in the mid-1960s: a lengthy essay in French, which then appeared in English translation nine years later,[5] and a short book on prayer originally requested by some friends in Delhi.In the past few years, however, the posthumous publication of his diary[6] and of a great many of his letters[7] has made possible a much more thorough grasp of the development of his thought, including his increasing dissatisfaction with the first book referred to above. What makes the choice of this author especially pertinent for the present investigation is that his sense of the divine mystery deepened precisely through his immersion in the religious life of another religious tradition, that of Hinduism, above all as found in the earliest Upanishads and in the more recent representatives of the *advaitic* (or "non-dualistic") doctrine of those ancient scriptures. If Le Saux did not formally develop the kind of "alliance" with non-Christian theists of which Rahner wrote, he nevertheless lived out such an alliance in his own life.

An Overview of Le Saux's Life

Henri Le Saux was born on August 30, 1910, in Saint-Briac, a small town on the north coast of Brittany. At the age of eleven, and with his parents' full encouragement, he entered a nearby minor seminary and later advanced to the major seminary at Rennes. An excellent student, he was slated to proceed to advanced theological studies in Rome, but in December 1928 he entered into correspondence with the novice-master at the Benedictine Abbey of Sainte Anne de Kergonan on the west coast of Brittany to explore the possibility of joining that community. A sentence from one of those letters sounds like a theme that in one way or another would characterize his deepest desire for the rest of his life: "What has drawn me [to the monastery] from the beginning, and what still leads me on, is the hope of finding there the presence of God more immediately than anywhere else."[8]

Accepted into the community in 1929, he made final profession in 1935, was ordained to the priesthood later in the same year, and began serving the monastery as librarian and assistant master of ceremonies. He was in the French army at the beginning of the Second World War, but his unit was forced to surrender to the German troops in 1940. Managing to escape his captors, he made his way back to Kergonan and moved with his fellow monks to another location when the monastery was requisitioned in 1942. Upon returning to Kergonan after the war, he again served as librarian and also gave classes to the novices in canon law and

Church history, with special emphasis on the writings of the Greek and Latin Fathers.

Already in 1934, however, references in his letters and diary reveal the beginnings of a call to India. Before the war he had received no encouragement from his abbot to pursue this call, but in 1945 he finally received permission to approach bishops in India who might be willing to receive him.

After a number of disappointments, he received a favorable response in 1947 from Bishop Mendonça of Tiruchirappalli in the south Indian state of Tamil Nadu. He had written the bishop asking permission to live an eremitical, contemplative life along the lines of early Christian monasticism and in close conformity with the tradition of Indian *sannyasa*. A French priest from Lyons, Jules Monchanin, had already been working in the diocese of Tiruchirappalli for some years and hoped eventually to adopt the same kind of life that Le Saux wrote about in his letter to Bishop Mendonça. Upon being shown the letter, Monchanin took it as an answer to his prayers for a kindred spirit with whom he could start an ashram. The two priests entered into correspondence and almost exactly a year later Le Saux arrived in India, where he would remain for the rest of his life.

During his first two years in the country, Le Saux visited many parishes and religious houses in Tamil Nadu and, regularly accompanied by Monchanin, also began visiting Hindu temples and ashrams. The most significant of the latter was situated at the foot of the sacred mountain of Arunachala, where the famous sage Sri Ramana Maharshi lived with his disciples. At first, Le Saux did not perceive anything special in Sri Ramana, but soon he sensed in the sage's quiet smile, in the profound concentration of his disciples, and in the Vedic chants sung each morning and evening "a call which pierced through everything, rent it in pieces and opened a mighty abyss.... New as [these experiences] were, their hold on me was already too strong for it ever to be possible for me to disown them."[9] Even after Sri Ramana died in 1950, Le Saux continued to frequent Arunachala, often spending weeks at a time in solitude in one of the caves that dot the sides of the mountain.

The dream of Monchanin and Le Saux to found a Christian ashram was realized in 1950, when they started living in simple huts at a site commonly called Shantivanam, along the banks of the Kavery River. In accordance with Indian tradition, Le Saux at this time took a new name, Abhishiktananda ("Bliss of the Anointed One"), by which he increasingly came to be known. Inquirers interested in joining the two men wrote or visited from time to time, but year after year these inquiries bore no fruit. In addition, the impractical temperament of Monchanin meant that most of the administrative work fell to Abhishiktananda. These factors, together with differences in theological outlook (Monchanin's thought seeming too "Greek" to Abhishiktananda, the latter's too "muddled" to Monchanin),[10] gradually led to a certain estrangement between the two men. Moreover, Abhishiktananda came to feel more and more drawn to north India, especially to the sources of the Ganges in the Himalayas. When Monchanin died in October 1957, only weeks after Abhishiktananda had completed an exhilarating seven-month tour of north India, Abhishiktananda felt all the more tempted to abandon Shantivanam and relocate in the north. As he later wrote to his sister Marie-Thérèse: "The Himalayas have conquered me! It is beside the Ganges that Shantivanam ought to be. I do not know if that will ever happen, but how splendid it would be!"[11] In fact, that never did happen, but Abhishiktananda did begin spending more and more time in the north, especially in a hermitage near the town of Uttarkashi besides the Ganges. He definitively left Shantivanam in late August 1968, leaving it in the hands of an English monk, Bede Griffiths, and two of the latter's companions.

Abhishiktananda thus came to spend the final five years of his life primarily in the Himalayas, though he would occasionally accept invitations to travel south for such purposes as giving retreats to religious communities, delivering addresses at conferences and seminars, or meeting with Church leaders to discuss ways of best implementing the directives and spirit of the Second Vatican Council. In fact, all during his years in India he had been lecturing and writing, not only occasional essays published in periodicals in India and France, but also books such as the two mentioned above. Two years before his death, he also had the joy of meeting someone who would truly become the disciple for whom he had always longed. Marc Chaduc, a French seminarian, had entered into correspondence with Abhishiktananda several years earlier and finally came to India to meet him in Delhi on October 21, 1971. In the following months Abhishiktananda devoted himself unsparingly to training Chaduc (as well as two Hindu disciples) in the ways of *sannyasa*, which Abhishiktananda saw as his own religious ideal and as the Indian counterpart to the total self-giving practiced by the earliest monks of Egypt, Palestine, and Syria.

On July 14, 1973, Abhishiktananda was briefly in Rishikesh, some fifty miles south of Uttarkashi, to buy provisions for Chaduc and himself. While running to catch a bus, he was stricken by a massive heart attack. For some time doctors, friends and religious sisters did all they could to nurse him back to health, but after five months of gradual recovery, marked by occasional relapses, he suffered another major attack and died late in the evening of December 7. He was buried the next day in the cemetery of the Divine Word Fathers in Indore, where his gravestone read simply: "Swami Abhishiktananda OSB / born 1910 / ordained 1935 / died 7.12.73." In 1995, his remains were transferred to the ashram he and Monchanin had founded at Shantivanam.

EVOLUTION IN ABHISHIKTANANDA'S
UNDERSTANDING OF GOD

From what was said above about young Henri Le Saux's theological training in French seminaries and a Benedictine monastery in the 1920s and 1930s, it is not surprising that his early understanding of God was shaped along the lines of what has more recently come to be known as "exclusivism," that is, the view that God can truly be known only through the Judeo-Christian revelation. [12] Attracted as the young monk was to India, the attraction was nevertheless not primarily in terms of what he might gain from exposure to the religious thought of that subcontinent, but rather in terms of what he could bring to the Indians. A year before leaving France, he wrote to Monchanin of his dream of founding a Benedictine community in India whose indigenous members would help "fashion a Christian India, as their elder brothers fashioned a Christian Europe." [13] A month after arriving in India, he wrote to his family that "the more I come to these Hindus, the more I feel them at the same time close to me in their loyal search for God and far from me in their psychological inability to admit that Christianity is the only authentic means of coming to God." [14]

It was not long, however, before Le Saux would no longer be able to use the adjective "only." It was above all his acquaintance with Sri Ramana Maharshi and the weeks he spent in solitude at Mount Arunachala in the early 1950s that led to a profound change in his whole religious stance. At first, he instinctively resisted these "powerful new experiences," finding it so difficult to incorporate them into his "previous mental structures," but the resistance was in vain: "Their hold on me was too strong for it ever to be possible for me to disown them." [15] At the heart of these experiences was what he came to call the *advaitic* experience or the Upanishadic experience—an overpowering sense of one's inmost self accompanied by the conviction that this self, the deepest core of one's being, is truly one with the Absolute, whether the latter be named God, Yahweh, Abba, or Brahman. One of Le Saux's clearest formulations of the nature of this experience was penned by him less than a month before his death, in a letter to his young French disciple:

> You are the only person, as well I know, to whom I have been able to say and to pass on everything, in words and beyond words.... You accepted the "*tabula rasa*" and from that *tabula rasa* the sparks flew. Yes, none of it was "mine" or "yours." But that "Greater One," whom you find lying behind myself and yourself, in not-other-than you or me. "The Father is greater than I." "I and the Father are one." The vision of Jesus recovers all its power when his Spirit....has "revealed" the depth of the *Aham* [I Am].[16]

The two sayings of Jesus quoted in that passage reveal the paradoxical nature of the experience, something of which Le Saux was fully aware. On the one hand there is a recognition of distinction between oneself and the Absolute ("The Father is greater than I"), and yet, at the same time, there is a sense of ultimate oneness inasmuch as one's own "I am" is experienced as not other (*a-dva*, "not two") than the inmost ground of all reality ("I and the Father are one").

Such experience altered Le Saux's understanding of his very vocation. Whereas he had come to India believing that living as a *sannyasi* would give effective Christian witness to Hindus, by 1952 he had come to the position that such a life of almost complete renunciation of secular possessions and desires was simply meaningful in itself, the outward expression of his sense that he was nearing the attainment of a radical monastic desire for the Absolute, against which everything else paled by comparison.[17] Writing at this time to his sister Marie-Thérèse (who had become a nun at

Kergonan, in this sense taking his place among the Benedictines in Brittany), he insisted that he was no longer "a missionary, but a poor Christian monk in the midst of Hindu monks."[18]

Sincerely desiring to remain true to his Christian faith even as he felt an ever stronger pull toward the doctrine of the Upanishads, he began working out ways in which his own evolving thought could form a bridge between the two faiths. Some of the essays he wrote in the 1950s and early 1960s were sent to theologians in France for their opinion prior to possible publication. There were diverse responses, generally positive from Henri de Lubac SJ, and A.-M. Henry OP, but so negative from P.-R. Regamey OP, and O. Cornelis, the latter a reader for the Cerf publishing house, that much of what he wrote at this period was published only posthumously, while a great deal remains unpublished to this day.[19]

One of his longest and most influential published works was *Sagesse hindoue, mystique chrétienne*, already mentioned as the work by which he has become best known in theological circles in the West. Here, Abhishiktananda clearly goes well beyond any exclusivist position to what he termed a "theology of fulfillment," in which *advaitic* experience and doctrine (and all other religious and spiritual experiences of the human race) are seen as converging upon the historical Christ and the Church. However, even at the time of its publication (1965), Abhishiktananda had already moved beyond that approach in his own thought. Six years after the appearance of the French original, he wrote (in what would eventually become the introduction to the posthumously published English translation) that the entire work was of an "introductory character," which had to "start from accepted positions, and then try to carry theological reflection a little further forward."[20] In letters written around the same time, he was even more critical of the book, saying that his limited revision of the French original in view of the English translation he was preparing with the assistance of

James Stuart was "only the patching up of an old wall. I would never have written it now."[21]

The basic problem was that upon arriving in India he had quickly moved beyond the (relatively mild) exclusivism of his formative years in France, had briefly adopted the position of a theology of fulfillment (still advocated years later in *Sagesse hindoue* apparently because he felt that was as far as he could go at the time and still get the work published), and then had come to a position that in today's terminology would be called pluralistic. Thus, already in 1954 he was confiding to his diary that "Christianity, Hinduism, Buddhism, etc., are not parallel, nor is each of them a successive step, Christianity being the definitive step. They are all *darsana* (perceptions) of the Beyond. Each is true in its own line."[22]

Perhaps the key term in that passage is "the Beyond," for it indicates that the fundamental impulse for this rapid conversion to a pluralistic position came from Abhishiktananda's experience and understanding of God in the light of his stays at Mount Arunachala and his reflection on the earliest Upanishads. The one to whom he had formerly prayed in the choir stalls of Sainte Anne de Kergonan was now forcefully experienced as not only the God of Abraham, Isaac, and Jacob, not only the Abba to whom Jesus taught his disciples to pray, but "the Beyond," the One who is indeed manifested in all the *namarupa* of the world religions but is not really comprehended by any of them.

Expressed thus, it might seem that Abhishiktananda is not saying anything different from what can be found in any traditional textbook of theology: that God's reality utterly transcends the powers of the human mind, that God is "wholly Other." But the crucial difference, certainly as far as Abhishiktananda himself understood the matter, is that for most theologians the incomprehensibility or unnameability of God "is still a concept, an idea—the apophatism of theology," whereas "only when the soul has undergone the experience that the Name beyond all names can be pronounced only in the silence of the Spirit does it become capable of that total openness which permits one to perceive the mystery in its sign."[23] Abhishiktananda had no doubt that he himself had gone beyond the level of concept to that of experience, first during his periods of solitude at Arunachala in the 1950s and later at various places in north India, at times when in the company of his disciple Marc Chaduc. These experiences, whether called *advaitic* or Upanishadic, were not, however, experiences of a personal God, but rather were regularly described by him as deep experiences of the self. They did not arise from any kind of ratiocination but from an utterly simple "awakening" to the fact that "I am" and that "the I which I pronounce today is identically the same as the I which I pronounced 10, 20, 60 years ago. As far back as I try to go into my memory, I find the same I, shining identical with itself, a sun always at its zenith."[24] To the real or hypothetical critics who wondered what could be deemed religious about such an experience (whose formulation might even sound utterly banal), Abhishiktananda's answer was usually phrased in terms either of the Gospel or the Upanishads, for he claimed that Jesus' own experience was truly *advaitic*:

> In Johannine terms, Jesus discovered that the I AM of Yahweh belonged to himself; or rather, putting it the other way round, it was in the brilliant light of his own I AM that he discovered the true meaning, total and unimaginable, of the name of Yahweh. To call God "Abba" is an equivalent in Semitic terms of *advaita*, the fundamental experience.[25]

At still other times, Abhishiktananda supported his position with references to Saint John of the Cross, as when he claimed that the *advaitic* experience, "though it avoids the notion and the name of God, draws man nearer to the divine mystery than any experience of God which depends on names, forms, notions, images and symbols. We may remember here the teaching of John of the

Cross and the drastic purification of all mental symbols which he calls the dark night of the soul." [26] So central did Abhishiktananda consider this experience that he once boldly wrote that "anything about God or the Word in any religion which is not based on the deep I-experience is bound to be simply 'notion,' not existential. From that awakening to self comes the awakening to God—and we discover marvelously that Christ is simply this awakening on a degree of purity rarely if ever reached by man." [27]

Similarly, he came to hold that the Church's primary call is that of bringing about "a spiritual awakening to God," even if in particular cases an individual's interpretation of the experience of awakening does not correspond to that of the Church. [28] It is obvious from such a claim how far Abhishiktananda had come in his thinking since the time he arrived in India with missionary intent. Before long, he was not shrinking even from using the word "relativity" to characterize the ways in which the various religions and philosophies of the world have tried to approach the fundamental questions of the mystery of life: From where do we come? Where are we going? What is our *raison d'être*?

Anyone truly confronting such questions will, like Abhishiktananda himself, feel "enveloped by mystery, mystery around him, mystery in front of him." Such a person may well attend to the answers offered by religion and philosophy, but one day he senses the relativity of it all. And then? *Ko'ham*? Who, what am I? Nothing that his reason has attained, not even reason guided by faith, can satisfy him any longer, nothing that people teach as rational, nothing that they claim to transmit as revealed. All that is relative in a constitutive way. "A person has in his very depths a thirst for the Absolute in itself.... His repose is not possible as long as this inextinguishable thirst remains unsatisfied." [29]

In Abhishiktananda's own life, it was only after reaching this point, asking the question *Ko'ham?* that had been put to him by Sri

Ramana Maharshi at Arunachala, that he awakened to the bed-rock experience of the self. The certainty that he eventually found therein did not occur all at once, for at first he felt utterly adrift, wondering whether he was either Christian or Hindu. But with the passing of time he more and more expressed himself in terms of confidently *knowing* the truth of what he had experienced. After a particularly powerful experience in mid-1972, he wrote to his young French disciple, "I think that now I shall no longer approach P. (or indeed anyone else) with the thought that *he knows* and that *I do not know*, for now I *do know, vedaham!*" [30] In a similar vein, somewhat earlier, he wrote to a friend in Switzerland: "Neither books nor lectures can convey this experience. You have to awake to another level of awareness.... I now *know* the Upanishad is true, *satyam*." [31]

"Knowing" that the Upanishads were true did not, however, lead Abhishiktananda to abandon the Christian tradition in which he had been raised. Clearly, from all that has been said above, he did indeed no longer see Christianity as the only authentic or even as the unquestionably most perfect way to God. He was especially wary of a tendency he perceived in Christianity to absolutize its symbols, as over against Hinduism's readiness to see itself tran-scended in the acosmic, aliturgical form of *sannyasa*. All the same, he recognized that the symbols, the *namarupa*, of each religion do have their rightful role, that there are "some great places—Sinai, Jordan, Tabor," and that "because we are flesh, we have great need of flesh and of place, precisely in order to release the total mystery of the flesh." [32] He considered it a great virtue of the Eastern reli-gions that they could teach Christians both "to recognize as *nama-rupa* all that previously we considered to be most sacred" and yet to recognize the value of these "names and forms." Those who learn this lesson from the East "have discovered another level of truth," in which "we find ourselves once more Christian, Hindu,

Buddhist, for each one has his own line of development, marked out already from his mother's lap. But we also have the 'smile.' Not a smile which looks down condescendingly from above, still less a smile of mockery, but one which is simply an opening out, like the flower unfolding its petals." [33]

It was with this kind of smile that Abhishiktananda lived out the final years of his life. Particularly precious to him during these years was the teaching of the Gospel about the centrality of love, which he saw not as some ethical duty imposed from without but as a most excellent and effective way of arriving at genuine awakening, since it is "love which releases man from the limitations of his ego and throws him into the arms of God and his brothers." [34] He made a point of insisting that "Jesus did not rack his brains to make a philosophy about his *advaita* with God…. He taught his people to live, simply but deeply, a life of loving union with their brothers—a union of self-giving without limit," a self-giving in which "the Absolute is found and lived with far greater truth than in Vedantin speculations." [35] And while he knew that the Gospel calls Christians to extend such love to everyone, he also knew that it is the poor and oppressed who have a special claim on it. Speaking of the poetic beauty of the Advent liturgy, he once lamented the fact that this easily "anesthetizes Christians, who are too often happy to repeat each year, 'He will come and will not delay,' while the poor look in vain for bread, shelter and respect. Advent is the cry of the poor, humiliated and frustrated, who are waiting for me, the Christian, to come to their help." [36] For Abhishiktananda these were not just pious musings; the poverty of so many people in India never ceased to touch him, and to the end of his life he continued to send help from his own meager funds to a family in Tamil Nadu who were in difficult circumstances.

Similar concern was extended to Abhishiktananda himself during his final illness, but there is no indication that his friends needed in any way to reconcile him with the prospect of death. The heart attack he suffered in the Rishikesh bazaar was the occasion of an experience that he unhesitatingly called "marvelous," for it was

> the discovery that the AWAKENING has nothing to do with any situation, even so-called life or so-called death; one is awake, and that is all. While I was waiting on my sidewalk, on the frontier of the two worlds, I was magnificently calm, for I AM, no matter in what world!....And this extra lease on life—for such it is—can only be used for living and sharing this discovery.[37]

In fact, he was so often prostrate with exhaustion during the final months of his life that very little direct sharing of the experience was possible; on many days he could do no more than lie in his bed, unable to meditate or concentrate, existing "like a beast before Thee" (Ps. 73:22, a verse he frequently quoted in his last letters). In any case, the "discovery" in Rishikesh was not utterly new but was of a piece with experiences that went back at least twenty years and that he had long been communicating as best he could through articles, books, letters, retreat conferences, private conversations, and other ways. In all this activity he was primarily trying "to pass on to the Christian world the honey which I gather in the Hindu world, and vice versa, however dislocating it may sometimes be."[38]

A Summary and Evaluation of Abhishiktananda's Theology

Although Abhishiktananda was often very critical of professional theologians, whose whole approach to the question of God he considered too "Greek," he himself definitely practiced theology in the basic sense of thinking and teaching about God. Moreover, he very much wanted to help bring about a renewed Christian theology, one that would be more open to the other world religions and more rooted in the experience of believers. What he actually said and wrote about God, however, might appear quite meager, for it is hard to find a thinker in the entire Christian tradition who was more thoroughly apophatic than he. Within a few years of his arrival in India, he had come to the conclusion that "the Church should be thought out in terms of the whole cosmic mystery and of the impenetrable mystery of God."[39]

Since this mystery is "beyond words," all "deductions and speculations fall short," for they necessarily operate on the level of *namarupa*, whereas "in every religion and in every religious experience there is a beyond, and it is precisely this 'beyond' that is our goal."[40] At times, one might well not even be able to address this "beyond" as "Thou," since in *advaitic* experience "God is no longer a HE about whom people dare to speak among themselves, nor even a THOU whose presence a person realizes as facing him."[41] Hence, "there may be days or periods of days when no 'Thou' to God can pass my lips, but that is quite normal, and there is no need to be worried about it. There are two mental states, each of them seeking desperately to express the unique *cit* of *sat* [awareness of reality]. And this freedom is what we have to insist on."[42]

Convinced that the mystery of God is "a cosmic mystery," Abhishiktananda was reluctant to compare in an evaluative sense the way it has been manifested in one religion as over against another. As a Christian, he did indeed pray to Christ, being "well aware that he is the most inward mystery, of which the Resurrection has caused all forms to explode."[43] But he did not want to limit this Christ to Jesus of Nazareth or even to the total Christ, head and members, of the Christian Church. Rather, it was "the cosmic Christ," identical with the *isvara* (manifested Lord) of Hindu faith, the *purusha* (archetypal human being) of the Upanishads. That being so, "why then call him only Jesus of Nazareth? Why say that it is Jesus of Nazareth whom others unknowingly call Shiva or Krishna? Why not rather say that Jesus is the theophany for us (Christians)....of that unnamable mystery of the Manifestation, always tending beyond itself, since Brahman transcends all its/his manifestations?"[44]

Abhishiktananda's reflections on the doctrine of the Trinity were also formulated against the background of this "unnamable mystery." According to him, "the Trinity is an experience, not a *theologoumenom*."[45] As such, at its originating moment, the experience cannot be disclosed by any word other than an exclamation of awe and wonder: "Ah!"[46] As soon as one reflects on the experience, one necessarily enters the realm of *namarupa*, and while the resulting formulations might even be called "magnificent," they have no absolute value and may even be misleading.

For this reason, Abhishiktananda himself became more and more reluctant to speak about such matters. In the final year of his life, he was invited to give some lectures on the Trinity at the Jesuit theological faculty in Delhi. He felt he could not refuse the invitation, since Delhi was not all that far from his hermitage, but he agreed to go only with misgivings: "I am a little anxious about these lectures requested by Delhi.... What can I say now? Lead them towards the 'open sea', with all moorings severed.... Nothing comes that is worth saying. When it comes to it, I shall have to be ready to speak without any particular preparation."[47] Clearly, Abhishiktananda was coming to practice more and more what he felt should be common in the Church as a whole: fewer words, more silence in the presence of the holy mystery.

When critiqued in the light of traditional Christian thought, Abhishiktananda's theology was in some obvious respects heterodox. He himself knew that much of what he wrote would not find acceptance on the part of other Christian thinkers. In a late letter, he candidly admitted, "I wonder if my thinking is on the right lines."[48] He was a pluralist years before this term became common and so anticipated many of the positions expressed, for example, in the book *The Myth of Christian Uniqueness* (which itself has already provoked a volume of critical rejoinders).[49] Abhishiktananda's manner of not merely distinguishing between the cosmic Christ and Jesus of Nazareth but sharply dichotomizing them (with Jesus being one of many authentic manifestations of the ineffable divine reality) cannot be expected to find acceptance in mainstream Catholic or Christian thought.

Moreover, those who hold that the formulations of traditional Western theology, however ultimately inadequate, nevertheless do provide a genuine access to truth will be uncomfortable with the very sharp dichotomy Abhishiktananda drew between experience and conceptualization, leading him to make such claims as that "the terms *Three Persons* and *Nature* have to be given up as misleading and, at least in translation, as wrong.... I think no real theology of the Trinity-Incarnation is possible as long as we do not turn back to the fundamental *anubhava* (experience) which they express."[50]

This "solution" of turning back to experience is simplistic. Abhishiktananda clearly believed that he himself had "turned back" in this way, but—despite the fact that he had a keen mind, a gift for finding *le mot juste*, and a desire for a genuinely Indian theology—he was unable to produce anything like a Trinitarian theology in his final years. (We have just seen his anxiety at having to speak on this subject at the Jesuit faculty in Delhi, and may also recall the fact that by this time he had largely repudiated the way he had gone about sketching such a theology in the final chapters of *Saccidananda*.[51]) This is not the most damning of criticisms; after all, not everyone needs to be a professional theologian. But of those who are called to this vocation, far more is required than being open to the fundamental *anubhava* of the divine mystery. Specifically, such persons must use their powers of conceptualization in a responsible and rigorous way without being daunted by Abhishiktananda's fear that the result of their efforts will likely be misleading if not downright wrong.

Abhishiktananda was very critical of the "Greek" heritage of the Christian Church, but in fact the theological formulations of any tradition (whether Semitic, Greek, Indian, Chinese, or whatever) will have both their strengths and their weaknesses. He was right in wanting to foster an Indian theology, but too harsh in his pejorative statements about the theology prevalent in the Western Church up to his time. How, after all, could anyone be so certain that the speculations of theologians like Saint Athanasius, Saint Basil, Saint Augustine, or Saint Thomas Aquinas on the Incarnation or the Trinity did not arise out of their own deep experience of these mysteries?

These remarks, however, do not mean that there is nothing of value in Abhishiktananda's work. I will highlight what I find to be four of the more positive features of his theology.

First, as noted several times already, one of the most prominent aspects of Abhishiktananda's thought is his emphasis on the incomprehensibility of God, an apophatic theme prominent already in the Patristic era in the works of such authors as Saint Gregory of Nyssa and Pseudo-Dionysius the Areopagite. In our own day, when awareness of the unimaginable vastness of the universe has been borne in upon us in ways inconceivable to earlier generations, it is scarcely possible for thoughtful believers to conceive of the Lord Jesus (or the Persons of the Trinity) seated in or above the highest of the heavenly spheres, as was still being done only a few centuries ago even by leading theologians. An understanding of God that does not provoke a schizophrenic split between oneself as a believer and oneself as a student of recent advances in cosmological science is surely a necessity today. God is unfathomable mystery, and Abhishiktananda was gifted with the ability to convey this not only in language commensurate with that used by academics but also in terms accessible to the most humble of believers, as when he wrote to a woman in Bombay: "Joy to you, to your husband, to your children. May it shed its rays on all! And don't worry about those who love the esoteric, who run around to ashrams and 'saints.' The discovery of the mystery is so much simpler than that. It is right beside you, in the opening of a flower, the song of a bird, the smile of a child!" [52]

A second point: Like the mystics of all times and all traditions, Abhishiktananda enjoyed a keen awareness of the self at the deepest level and found in the Upanishads a simple, lucid description of such awareness. Here we are at the heart of his teaching. He once wrote: "I am always frightened of people stopping at the 'negative' aspect of my message (no institutions, etc.), whereas all negations....gain their meaning only in this breakthrough to the depth of the I." [53] This, too, is of great significance for our time. As the respected religious philosopher Louis Dupré has written:

> the ultimate message of the mystic about the nature of self-hood is that the self is *essentially* more than a mere self, that transcendence belongs to its nature as much as the act through which it is imminent to itself.... The general trend of our civilization during the last centuries...has been to reduce the self to its most immediate and lowest common denominator. But for this restriction we pay the price of an all pervading feeling of unfulfillment and, indeed, of dehumanization." [54]

In a mystic like Abhishiktananda one finds just the opposite of any such feeling of unfulfillment. Even in times of considerable anguish, when he felt that he had lost his way at that turbulent boundary "where the two oceans (Hinduism and Christianity) mingle their waters in a dangerous and troubling way," [55] he never lapsed into any lethargic state of felt unfulfillment. Instead, he remained faithful to the single-minded quest for the Absolute that had first drawn him to monastic life. His fidelity was rewarded, for the final years of his life were generally marked by a calm but radiant joy altogether evident in photographs of him taken at that time. Letters that he wrote after his heart attack in Rishikesh also reveal with all possible clarity the deep sense of centeredness to which his admittedly singular journey had brought him.

Third, Abhishiktananda's contention that a truly religious person will not always be able to address God as "Thou," since there are two "mental states" involved and each must be given its due, might at first hearing seem strange. It is, however, very much in accord with the thought of many leading theologians. Gordon D. Kaufman, for example, has used the contrasting terms "metaphysical" and "mythic" to describe these two approaches:

> If one emphasizes only the mythic and anthropomorphic characterizations that make God religiously attractive, one increasingly moves away from plausible metaphysical talk about God...; but conversely, if one emphasizes abstract metaphysical concepts about a "cosmic movement" toward, or "cosmic ground" of our humanity, to the exclusion of more anthropomorphic and personalistic imagery, the concept loses its religious power and attractiveness as a focus for devotion and orientation. However difficult it may be to do so, the mythic and metaphysical dimensions...must be held together.[56]

Others have distinguished between "first order-language," appropriate for corporate worship, in which God may be addressed as "Shepherd of the flock" or "loving Father," and "second-order language," where the impersonal terminology of "absolute being" or *ipsum esse subsistens* would be in order.[57] Seen in the light of such texts, Abhishiktananda's reflections about God as "Thou" and "It" may more readily be understood and appreciated.

Last, there was in Abhishiktananda a lived awareness that the mystery of God as found in one's inmost self brings about a sense of freedom that is as rare as it is attractive. Writing to a Carmelite nun in the late 1960s, he said that "the deep reason for the present crisis [in the Church] is the exaltation of human laws above the Lord and of theology above experience of God." [58] Abhishiktananda in no sense scorned human laws, nor was he given to whimsical or arbitrary behavior. In *sannyasa* he did, however, find "the outward expression of man's ultimate freedom in his innermost being," [59] a freedom that allowed him, for example, to see possibilities for interfaith worship beyond that practiced with Christians of other denominations. Moreover, he approached formal "external dialogue" with Hindus in a way that clearly recognized that there is an equally important "silent interior dialogue" that must take place as each participant becomes "stimulated by the new vistas of thought which the dialogue opens up." [60] He did not shrink from giving expression to these new vistas, at least in his letters if not always in his published essays. While the resulting texts may be too extreme and unhelpful for many readers (and so ought not to be recommended *carte blanche*), persons of religious sensitivity and theological acumen can have their own interior dialogue fruitfully challenged by the reflections of this singularly honest thinker. He knew that his way was not for everyone, but he also knew that for some it could be imperative:

> Vedantin experience just as much drains people and is just as dangerous as drugs or psychoanalysis.... We should only allow very strong people to get involved with it.... It is probably better for most people to pass the *Shakti* (God's active power) by than to be a carrier of it without realizing it. For some are capable of it. It is for them that I should like to have a place beside the Ganges to receive them. [61]

Abhishiktananda did not live long enough to have such a place built next to the sacred river. But he also knew that earthly geography is not ultimately important. He often said that the Indian experience could be had anywhere: "India is wherever you find the Lord of the innermost depth, the Lord of the *Guha*. And the Cave is the deepest center of the heart and the deepest center of the Father's heart. Live there, whatever may be your circumstances." [62]

It was in that Cave that Abhishiktananda was convinced he had found the God whose mystery enveloped him and the entire universe, and it is on this discovery that all his written and spoken words focused. I believe Abhishiktananda's thought can—in the words of Karl Rahner quoted in my opening paragraph—help overcome "the inadequacy of our theism" and so show "how people today in all seriousness can have a living faith in God."

9

SWAMI ABHISHIKTANANDA
THEOLOGIAN OF INTERCULTURATION

Antony Kalliath CMI

Father Antony Kalliath is Secretary of the Indian Theological Association and professor at the National Biblical Catechetical and Liturgical Center in Bangalore. This chapter first appeared in number 20 (November 1999) of SETU, the Bulletin of the Abhishiktananda Society.

At the threshold of the third millennium, the world community is frantically searching for convincing models that can give direction and consistency to the future evolution of the coming generation. In the first and second millennia, there were generally accepted frameworks (e.g., the classical vision of the first millennium, the enlightenment model of the second millennium) that supplied consistency and character to humanity's general perception and interpretation of reality. Today, while humanity is struggling to face up to a pluralistic culture, we do not find any paradigm that can universally be applied or accepted. Rather, we find confusing trends and conflicting models cohabiting in an inordinate mutual accommodation (globalization and cultural nationalism; dialogue among religions and religious fundamentalism; socialist economies and capitalist markets). Coming to the religious spectrum today, we do not find any particular faith having complete hold over its adherents as used to be the case in the past; there seem to be many centers of meaning in the universe of faith. The movements of unity and forces of fragmentation coexist and influence people in a nebulous and ambivalent manner. Futurists are quite vague and evasive concerning what is in the offing. A sense of unpredictability and uncertainty pervades the collective consciousness concerning what will unfold in the third millennium.

However it seems that the most crucial challenge of this millennium will be in terms of a pluralist culture in which the focus will be on plurality in order to safeguard unity. That is to say, we will be challenged to develop a cultural philosophy and political system in which various cultural and ethnic identities and religious traditions are not merely respected but creatively interact and interface with one another in a pluralistic vision and paradigm.

In the process, what is needed is not merely inculturation or adaptation but an interculturation that may not necessarily lead to a third reality. Interculturation implies a composite cultural consciousness in which one is very much rooted in one's beliefs and faith but is at the same time related to the partner's belief systems and philosophies in a creative contemplation, more in terms of experience than of abstract categories. Abhishiktananda calls this pluralistic framework a "bridge consciousness." It is more a consciousness of plurality in unity than of unity in plurality. Once this consciousness is achieved at the depth of one's being, it will be easier to develop a culture of collaboration and dialogue among religions at the phenomenal level without confusions and conflict. Today many consider Swami Abhishiktananda to have been a prophet and pioneer of a fine embodiment of interreligious consciousness, especially in the realm of Hindu–Christian meeting. Hence he is a challenging model for the coming millennium, which will be characterized by pluralistic values in terms of interculturation.

Henri Le Saux was born into a pious Catholic family on August 30, 1910, at Saint Briac, a small town on the north coast of Brittany. During his seminary studies, he was profoundly drawn to monastic life and eventually entered the novitiate at Sainte-Anne de Kergonan in 1929. He made his final vows on May 30, 1935, and was ordained a priest in the same year.[1] Early in his monastic life he became fascinated with India, or rather, spiritually attracted to India. In one of his letters to Father Monchanin, his future co-worker, Le Saux wrote, "I deeply love holy India [and] her call makes my heart ache." "I am scared and feel crushed, but the call of India is deep in me, inscribed as it is on my inmost self."[2]

Dom Henri Le Saux left France for India on July 26, 1948, and disembarked at Colombo (Sri Lanka) on August 15. On the next day he arrived at Madras by ship. The following period of twenty-five years, culminating in his death on December 7, 1973, was an exciting phase of his intense search into the mystery of Hindu–Christian dialogue.

METHODOLOGY

The methodology adopted by Abhishiktananda in his experiment with Hinduism was existential and experiential to the core. He totally relied on Indian spiritual means (*sadhanas*) to achieve his experiential meeting with the Hindu genius. Indian *sadhanas* are generally classified under three titles: *bhaaktimarga* (means of devotion); *karmamarga* (means of action); *jnanamarga* (means of knowledge). Abhishiktananda mainly relied on *jnanamarga* of Upanishadic *advaita* in his enquiry.

To situate himself radically in an Indian ambience of self-enquiry, Abhishiktananda, along with Father Monchanin, who was then a missionary in Tamil Nadu, founded Saccidananda Ashram (Shantivanam) in 1950. Living there, Abhishiktananda entered into the dynamics and practice of Indian s*adhanas*. However, later he had to forsake his ashram in favor of the acosmic life in the Himalayas, the supreme expression of solitude and asceticism to which s*adhanas* ultimately lead the true seeker.

THEOLOGICAL VISION

The fundamental fascination of Swamiji, like that of the sages of Eternal India, is the mystery of Being. His writings are an attempt to peer at his own intense experience of Being. He tries to comprehend the mystery of Being in the paradigm of the Cycle of Being, which, however, implies no cyclic movement. Swamiji interprets the Christ-Event as the *exemplar par excellence* of the Ideal of the Cycle of Being.[3] According to Abhishiktananda, the key to understanding the mystery of the Christ-Event is what Jesus said: "I have come from the Father and I return to the Father." This *coming* and *returning* of the Word is the birth and rebirth of Being. Every human being, endowed with self-awareness, can become conscious of this mystery of the birth-rebirth of Being in a profound way in his or her own self (*atman*), the interior core and ground of being. Abhishiktananda is of the opinion that Hindu–Christian *meeting* has to first take place at the plane of rebirth—the process of the return of the Word to the bosom of the Father, one's awakening to the Self (*svayam-jyoti*).

In his writings, Abhishiktananda always stresses that Truth is not conceptual; it is simply awakening—*jyoti* (glow). Abhishiktananda reaches this Truth by responding to the irrepressible call of *advaita*. He makes a radical decision of unconditional submission to the call of *advaita* even at the risk of "bracketing out" (*epoché*) his Christian presuppositions for a short period. Subsequently, he begins to interpret the Christian self-understanding in terms of the *advaitic* awakening. At the *atman* level, he finds reconciliation between *advaita* and Christian experience of God, though not conceptually. Henceforth, the Christian *mythos* has meaning only at the level of *namarupa* in his vision and experience. In the *advaitic* awakening, as he writes in his journal, "I simply find myself profoundly Hindu and Christian at the same time."[4]

Abhishiktananda fundamentally interprets *advaitic* awakening in terms of God's presence to Himself—I AM. The human person enters the divine presence in the mystery of the Self. "This presence is entirely mine, founded in me, fixed in me, gushing out from the very depth of my presence to myself."[5] According to him, all our attempts to understand God gush out from the fundamental mystery of human being—"I am" *(aham asmi)*. So awakening to Self is awakening to God in the theological vision of Abhishiktananda.[6]

JESUS CHRIST IN SWAMIJI'S AWAKENING

If the unconditional surrender to the call of *advaita* makes Abhishiktananda transcend his Christian moorings and *mythos*, what can we say about his attitude toward Jesus Christ? More precisely, if self-awakening is awakening to God, is the reality of Jesus of Nazareth necessarily part of the God-experience of Abhishiktananda?

What we can infer from his journal and other writings is that Abhishiktananda tries to understand Jesus Christ in terms of the mystery of Guru; he develops a Guru Christology. That is to say, Christ is encountered in the mystery of every human being—I AM. This does not imply that Abhishiktananda diminishes the value of Jesus of Nazareth. What Abhishiktananda emphasizes is the higher level in which Jesus lived before the Father, mute and silent—Jesus simply gazed at the Father. This silence is the "tension" of the being to the Self, the Father—the mystery of Christ. Abhishiktananda writes in his journal, "This fundamental experience of 'I am' which lifts Jesus from every ego and makes him the one who is no more than the 'tension' towards the Father, towards his fellow being."[7] Therefore, Jesus' name is the saving name (Supername) because it helps his followers to participate in this tension toward the Self (Father).

Abhishiktananda explains the meaning of "Jesus" in the spectrum of self-awakening in the following way: In the beginning (*en arché*) God said to himself: *I am.* This *aham asmi* is the *verbum,* the origin of consciousness, outside time and space. "Christ is the total transparency of the *aham asmi* to which I am awakened in the principle of my consciousness. Christ—if he means anything to me—is the very mystery of this awakening to me.... Christ is the revelation of my *aham*, of my *paraspara* (reciprocity) with every consciousness, every awakening." Hence Abhishiktananda says, "Jesus is not merely an idea.... But the very mystery of Jesus is to be discovered in self. Above all [Jesus] is not a Christological *gnosis*, but the I AM that I can only know in my AHAM."[8]

For him the name I AM, which Jesus applies to himself (John 8:22), is the key to his mystery. The discovery of this Name (in the depth of one's own I AM) is truly salvation for each one of us.[9] Jesus remained as his inviolable Guru in the process of his self-realization. He writes, "If I say that I believe in Christ, that means that Christ is God for me. God-for-me, because there is no abstract God.... Jesus is God's face turned toward man and man's face turned toward God."[10]

HINDU–CHRISTIAN MEETING

The fundamental position of Abhishiktananda regarding the problematic of Hindu–Christian meeting is that it should not primarily be considered as an encounter between two religions. Rather, it is to be a mutual soul-to-soul *meeting* of two fundamental experiences of humankind at the most profound level of being, despite the basic strains between them on the conceptual level. Abhishiktananda says that the tension between *advaita* and Christianity is insoluble because the supreme experience of Christianity—Trinity—is the mystery of faith. This is of a quite different order when compared with a Hindu *jnani*'s direct realization of being. The plane of the experience of *advaita* and that of faith cannot meet each other. The gulf between them, in this sense, is very real.

Nevertheless, Abhishiktananda holds that to be a disciple of Jesus, that is, to participate in the experience of Jesus—I AM—"does not mean that one needs to be a member of a sociological group. The experience of 'I AM' is the fundamental experience of every human being in the *Cave of the Heart*. Such a meeting cannot be named, located or seen and is without any form (*arupa, anama, alinga, avyakta*); it is the unique splendor of the Self. So India in her depths calls to the Church; for it is only in the depth that the marvelous encounter will manifest itself." [11]

Hindu–Christian meeting is never a mere academic or theological concern for Abhishiktananda. It belongs to the very religious fiber of his being. He himself is torn between the "extreme borders where the two Oceans (Hinduism and Christianity) mingle their waters dangerously." [12] Remaining there, he considers himself profoundly Hindu and Christian at once. About this double loyalty he says, "It is precisely this being torn apart between *advaita* and Christianity which enables me to live the fundamental experience and to express its mystery to some extent." [13]

The fundamental experience, according to him, is like a profound mutation. For his part, he decides to be the bearer of this tension rather than to stay out of it. Abhishiktananda thinks that this border experience has to go on for some time in the Church before a theological crystallization of the meeting takes place in the future. Being the bearer of this border-experience, Abhishiktananda regards himself as a bridge between these two fundamental experiences of humanity—a bridge that unifies the frontiers. To be such a bridge, he thinks is his vocation. [14]

THE MEANING OF SELF-AWAKENING

Abhishiktananda writes in his journal on May 11, 1972: "The experience of the Upanishads is true. *I know it.*"[15] Though we find such a clear statement very late (just one year before his death), *advaita* has been the inner bedrock of his life and thinking. Evidently, this assertion is more a personal and experiential confession than an intellectual statement. The question is how Abhishiktananda intends the insertion of his Christian experience of God in this affirmation.

For Abhishiktananda, *advaita* is neither monism nor dualism. It means the mystery of being surging toward its Source. This surge corresponds to the ontological tension between the two Poles of Reality—One and Many. This ontological tension is *advaitic*, for it is the co-incidence of One and Many or the simultaneity of the Non-Manifest and Manifest. Endowed with intellect, only a human being can become aware of this tension at the depth of one's being (*atman*) in a profound way. The theological as well as experiential *locus* of Abhishiktananda's statement—the experience of the Upanishads is true—is to be sought precisely in his intense awareness of this ontological movement of being in the realm of his subjectivity (*aham asmi*). I think it is in this sense that Abhishiktananda appropriates or makes the insertion of the Upanishadic *advaita* into his Christian consciousness.[16]

In Abhishiktananda's awakening, *advaita* is only the inner experiential *point de départ* for entering into the mystery of God: *advaita* is not the final state of realization. So he speaks of a trans-*advaita* that we can only witness in a profound interior solitude. However, he considers that the Christian revelation is a better way of understanding this trans-*advaita* realm in the mysteries of Trinity and Love.

In the *advaitic* fire, Abhishiktananda gives primary importance to the trans-historicity of Christian experience. In different words, he tried to appropriate Jesus existentially in the "now" more than in the "historical." It should be said that the historical dimension of the Christian faith experience was somehow overshadowed or rather marginalized when Abhishiktananda increasingly interpreted Jesus' mystery in terms of *atman* experience.

At this juncture note should be taken of the frequent criticism that Abhishiktananda underestimated the importance of the mediation of concepts by emphasizing the primacy of experience. Abhishiktananda himself agreed with that criticism. But at the same time one should not miss Swamiji's emphasis in this regard. First of all, Abhishiktananda is of the opinion that Western language is shut in, one-dimensional, and very much desacralized. So he thinks that "to harmonize....the deep experience and its 'expression,'....the Mediterranean 'expression' is terribly unsatisfying if not misleading." According to him, "What is horrifying in theology and Canon Law is the treatment of *namarupa* as absolutes." [17]

What Abhishiktananda insists upon is that all our dogmas must be considered as the *upasana* (meditation) or *vidya* (knowledge) of the Upanishads. What we discern here is that Abhishiktananda is more a metaphysician than a philosopher in the matter of subjecting experience to interpretation and mediation. He does not share his awakening as a philosophy. A metaphysician is more concerned "with matters which cannot be publically proved but can only be demonstrated, that is, made intelligible by analogy." [18] Hence Abhishiktananda's texts can be misunderstood if they are separated from his pursuit and quest.

From a Western rational theological perspective, as some may point out, Swamiji could not succeed in subjecting his awakening to the mediation of concepts. According to Gregory of Nazianzus, the best theologian is not the one who gives a systematic and logical account of his theme, but the one who "assembles more of Truth's image and shadow" and thus moves beyond the boundaries of pure rationality.[19] This does not mean abandoning rationality, but at the same time one should not favor reductionism of theology to rationality. Abhishiktananda's writings are more of Truth's images and shadows of the mystery of Hindu–Christian dialogue. In this sense, he is a prophet as well as a pioneer theologian in the field of interfaith theology.

Communication in depth across the boundaries of one's religious faith is what is most important in fashioning the destinies of future humanity.[20] John Dunne says, "The holy man of our time, it seems, is not a figure like [the founder of] a world religion, but a figure like Gandhi, a man who passes over by sympathetic understanding from his own religion to other religions, and comes back again with new insight to his own. "Passing over and coming back, it seems, is the spiritual adventure of our time."[21]

In today's world of religious pluralism, a spirit of spiritual adventure is imperative for the greater cohesion and harmony of various religions and cultures. But this passing over has to be realized first at the depth level. Abhishiktananda used to say that the seed should be sown as deeply as possible so that the plant may be deep-rooted in the soil for a lasting and fruitful growth. Through a radical encounter with Hinduism, Abhishiktananda has given to humanity a profound model of interculturation and thus of how to be holy in an ethos of pluralist vision, which will be the hallmark of the new millennium.

10

AN INTRODUCTION TO THE DIARY
OF SWAMI ABHISHIKTANADA

Bettina Bäumer

*This chapter first appeared in number 20 (November 1999)
of* SETU, the *Bulletin of the Abhishiktananda Society. It was
a talk that was given at a book discussion on March 29 of
the same year at India International Centre, New Delhi, to
mark the appearance of the English translation of Swami
Abhishiktananda's diary,* Ascent to the Depth of the Heart.

It has taken a long time for the spiritual diary of Swami
Abhishiktananda to see the light of day in an English translation.[1] The French original was published in 1986, that too after a
gap of thirteen years following his death. In the meanwhile, some
of us who were involved in the process of editing and translating
expressed doubts as to whether the content of the diary would still
be relevant by the time it came out in English. We live in a fast-
moving time, when concerns and interests are changing almost
daily. Would the reflections and experiences of a French monk and
Indian *sannyasi* not be outdated and appear old fashioned as we
move into the third millennium?

The contrary seems to be true. In India and outside India.
Swami Abhishiktananda is hailed as a pioneer in the intercultural and interreligious scene of our time. Many people who are
in search of a spirituality that is open to other traditions without
negating their own have turned to Swami Abhishiktananda as a

guiding light. Without wanting to become a thinker defending religious pluralism, Swamiji has demonstrated with his life what it means not only to respect other religious traditions but to become deeply involved in them. As he said—almost with a sigh—at the beginning of his stay in Tamil Nadu, "I have two loves."

What is the relevance of a diary as compared to the books written by the same author? In books an author pursues a specific topic and purpose, with the necessary literary and academic expression. Most of Swamiji's books are mainly meant to help Christians understand the deep spiritual values of India and the convergences between Hindu and Christian thought and experience. In his diary he enters into dialogue with himself, without any fear or inhibition and without any intention other than pouring out his deepest thoughts and experiences. Thus, the diary is an authentic witness to the inner struggles and tensions as well as to the overwhelming discoveries of a life lived at the confluence, the *sangam,* of two spiritual traditions and cultures. As Raimon Panikkar wrote in his introduction to the diary:

> We witness the development of a soul's archetypes under the influence of two different cultures. To live at the meeting point of several traditions is the destiny of a large portion of the human race. For very many people it is hardly possible any longer to feel at home in a single culture. To camp out in the workshops of technology does not answer to human aspirations. A new insight is required. This is where Abhishiktananda's experience seems to me to be of great importance (p. xvi).

Much of the present-day controversy between religions in India and elsewhere stems from the simplistic view of assuming that religions are closed boxes and that people belong to one or the other of these boxes without interaction and mutual influence. If, on the one hand, we see evidence of this so-called fundamentalist attitude to religions, on the other, we have abundant evidence—mainly in the West—of a kind of religious supermarket where one can "pick and choose" from any religious tradition according to one's personal liking.

Swami Abhishiktananda's diary is most relevant in this present, often confused, situation. It allows us, so to speak, a look into a laboratory of spiritual alchemy. It allows us to witness the process of a deep inner transformation. After spending nineteen years in a strict Benedictine monastery in France, Henri Le Saux comes in contact with Indian spirituality; immerses himself in the land, the culture, and the people of Tamil Nadu, and, most important, meets Sri Ramana Maharshi, in whom he saw the archetypal *rishi* of India. This meeting had such a deep impact on Le Saux that it brought him under the inexorable spell of *advaita*, not as a philosophy but as an experience:

> This ideal which is most profoundly mine—the one to which unconsciously everything in me is referred—is that of *Ramana*....such a perfect example of Vedanta—and this idea of Ramana would not have been able to root itself at such a depth in my psyche if it had not encountered a call already expressed, a *"surfacing"* and "awakening" (July 2, 1971, p. 328).

In his own inner self began what Panikkar calls the "intra-religious dialogue," with all its doubts, struggles, and insights. "From now on I have tasted too much of *advaita* to be able to recover the 'Gregorian' peace of a Christian monk. Long ago I tasted too much of that 'Gregorian' peace not to be anguished in the midst of my *advaita*" (September 27, 1953, p. 74). He takes both traditions, the Hindu and the Christian, seriously in all their implications, and yet, by this very encounter they become relativized, and ultimately transcended. In 1953, he is in the middle of this process when he writes:

Beneath the human wrapping there is something very much deeper in both of these attachments which torments me and tears me apart—on the final boundary where the two oceans (Hinduism and Christianity) mix their waters dangerously and disturbingly together.

What compass can hereafter give direction to one who is standing right at the Pole? Where is the East and where is the West? Where does the sun rise and where does it set in a six month day and a six month night? He has *transcended* all direction—so it is with one who has penetrated to the Self (September 27, 1953, p. 74).

The process of penetrating to the self helped Abhishiktananda to deepen both experiences and to discover convergences at the level of the self, of the ultimate: "I," *aham*. He discovered that the self-identity of any religious tradition and therefore of the believers is very much bound to the archetypes in which this religion has developed and expressed itself:

Loyalty to a tradition is a psychological/mythical means of living in loyalty to oneself—for the deepest aspect of one's being, of the psyche, is necessarily lived under the archetype of the "primordial," of the *earlier* in time. And a sudden discovery risks making everything explode—with bits that would break up and be lost all over the solar system or the Milky Way.

Dogmas have the value of *upasana*, including the fundamental dogmas of the divinity of Christ and of his trinitarian pre-existence. They are all "detours" which prepare for the *awakening*. Not so much detours, as tracks, going round the mountain, which climbs up in a spiral toward the peak (July 2, 1971, pp. 328–329).

In Vedanta he found a wonderful terminology to describe the limitations that religions impose upon the Absolute; they are all *namarupa*, human identification with particular names and forms. In the light of experience, the different expressions lose their importance. "We take our verbalizations much too seriously. They are not decisive either for reality or for our experiences" (June 11, 1972, p. 356). This is so because

> Concepts are dualistic and therefore falsify everything that they claim to express about what is beyond *dvandvas*. The *dvandva* Man/God in Jesus to start with, the *dvandva* sin/virtue, salvation/damnation. When Naciketas asks Yama what is beyond religious law and irreligion [*dharma/adharma*], beyond made and not made [*krita/akrita*], etc., Yama simply answers with OM! Truth cannot be formulated, at least at the luminous apex where all its splendor is concentrated (April 2, 1972, p. 342).

It is not an anti-intellectualistic attitude that makes Swamiji criticize all formulations and dogmas. He was too much aware of theology and philosophy, as the diary itself witnesses. But he wants to stress again and again that all concepts, even the most sublime theological concepts of any tradition, are bound to the culture and historical situation from which they sprang. They have their real meaning only at a certain level of consciousness; otherwise they are misleading. Seen from outside the tradition they will be misunderstood. It is therefore not a question of finding better concepts and more developed theologies, but of getting at the very source of these concepts. In the light of the *advaitic* experience, which for Swamiji was the acme of religion, all formulations explode.

CHRISTIANITY AND ADVAITA

> Neither opposition nor incompatibility—two different levels. *Advaita* is not something that conflicts with anything else at all. It is not a philosophy—but an existential experience (*anubhava*). The whole formulation of Christianity is valid in its own order, the order of manifestation (*vyavaharika*) (and so, provisional), and not of the Absolute (*paramarthika*). The Christian *darsana* (perception) is no doubt opposed to the Vedantin

darsana, but this merely at the doctrinal level. No formulation, not even that of *advaita*, can claim to be *paramartha* (October 23, 1970, p. 322)....

But the very condition of rejecting the formulas of "religions" is the disappearance of the ego who would otherwise assume a false position. So long as *I* have not disappeared, it is vain and dangerous to speak so much about *advaita* (p. 323).

Therefore his problem with the *concept* of God:

For several millennia humanity has, on the whole expressed its religious perception around the archetype of God (*theos*), which little by little took the place of the much less definite archetype, "gods" (*theoi*), the culmination of the religious evolution of the Neolithic era of humanity.

The archetype *theos* functions less and less well, at our end of the Neolithic era, as a way of expressing, focusing, grounding, etc., the "religious sense" (a convenient term, even if questionable) of modern people. The modern atheist (*a-theos*) is only opposed to the archetype *theos*, and not to the *mystery* that is expressed through *theos*—except insofar as the official *theoi* (theists) have done all they could to mix up the mystery and the archetype (November 24, 1970, p. 323).

Ultimately, the theoretical and practical conflicts between religious traditions get resolved only in the light of an illuminating experience. Abhishiktananda uses the simile of the light of the sun and stumps of candles when he emerges from a transforming experience that brought him to the verge of death in 1972:

I have a feeling that either I have nothing any longer to do here, *iha!* Or that I have nothing more to bear witness to except the fullness of light. All the *namarupas*, Hindu as well as Christian, are stumps of candle that we light at high noon—while the sun is at its zenith!

That purusha of glory (*tejas*) is to be found. I am he! (*So 'ham asmi*).

When the *tejas* is too strong, even the awakening, even sight disappears—how much more attentiveness to things!

It is deep sleep (*sushupti*) or else it is death—or else the cutting of the knots of the heart, the great death. It is the reaching of the sun in the *sahasrara*. It is the reuniting of the two purushas, that of the right eye and that of the sun. And it is only ONE!

It is being carried off to the place of the self, where one is oneself, pure light, supreme light (*param jyoti*)—pure being "*sati sampanna*" (immersed in being)—pure sun (*aditya*), pure life (*prana*) (June 10, 1972, p. 355).

In this light he can find wonderful correspondences between the Upanishads and the Gospel, without denying their difference: "The Gospel is centered on a person. The Upanishads on an experience" (p. 354).

His *sadguru* remained Christ, but

Christ loses nothing of his true greatness when he is freed from the false forms of greatness with which myths and theological reflection have decked him out. Jesus is the marvelous epiphany of the mystery of Man, of the Purusha, the mystery of every human being, as were the Buddha and Ramana and so many others. He is the mystery of the Purusha who is seeking himself in the cosmos. His epiphany is strongly marked by the time and place of his appearance in the flesh!! (January 2, 1973, p. 367).

He now recognizes the same mystery under the different names and forms in which it has been worshipped. "I recognize this mystery, which I have always adored under the symbol of Christ, in the myths of Narayana, Prajapati, Shiva, Purusha, Krishna, Rama, etc. This same mystery" (July 24, 1971, p. 332).

Finally, it is

This staggering discovery, new each time, after the manner of a dream, always the same and always new!—that what I had projected outside myself into a sphere that was divine, eternal, etc., and had adored, loved, and so on, is the mystery of my own being—*sa eshah purusha so 'ham, so 'ham asmi!* That Person yonder (in the sun)—I am he!" (Isa Upanishad, 16) (July 22, 1971, p. 331).

In this perspective we can hope with Raimon Panikkar that something of that awakening be experienced by everyone who takes up this diary, starting from what he or she already knows (p. x).

Swami Abhishiktananda's diary is above all a document of the authentic experience of one who has spiritually moved "in both worlds, the East and the West," as his favorite Keshisukta of the Rig-Veda (X,136) says, because he has been "moved by the Wind," by Vayu, by the Spirit, from within, to discover "the hidden connection" that only the inner vision can reveal.

THE UNITY OF RELIGIONS

Karan Singh

Dr. Karan Singh, member of Parliament and one of the lead-
ing Hindus in interreligious dialogue, chaired the book discus-
sion that took place on March 29, 1999, at India International
Centre, New Delhi, to mark the appearance of the English
translation of Swami Abhishiktananda's diary, Ascent to the
Depth of the Heart. *His introductory and concluding remarks*
are brought together in this chapter. They first appeared
in number 20 (November 1999) SETU, *the Bulletin of the*
Abhishiktananda Society.

The year 1893 marked the beginning of interfaith dialogue.
Uninvited, Swami Vivekananda turned up at the World
Parliament of Religions in Chicago and left his mark with an
historic address. Exactly one hundred years later, in 1993, six
thousand delegates again gathered in Chicago. I led the Indian
delegation.

According to both the Marxian and Western liberal views, religion was supposed to have lost its relevance. But it has had its
abiding impact on people for good and bad. Cathedrals, temples of
South India, etc., remind one of the influence of religion. It is also
a fact that many people have been killed in the course of history
in the name of religion. A strong religious factor is involved in the
war that is going on in Yugoslavia.

The context of India's pluralistic culture and multi-religious setting provides ample opportunity for the interfaith movement. Interreligious dialogue forms a part of this movement. One of the components of it is the Hindu–Christian dialogue. Two factors have contributed to it. One is that some Christians—Sri Krishna Prem and Swami Subramaniam—became Hindu swamis. The second is that some Christians, remaining loyal to their religions, have plunged into Hindu spirituality. Among these latter, Swami Abhishiktananda stands out. Once he came to India in 1948 he never went back. Having the *darshan* of Ramana Maharshi had a great influence on him.

Then we have Bede Griffiths, who took over the ashram at Shantivanam near Tiruchirapalli from Swami Abhishiktananda. Raimon Panikkar, with whom many of us are familiar, may be called a Christian-Hindu or Hindu–Christian. He has made his own translation of the Veda, titled *Mantra Manjari*, which is a significant contribution to the quest of modern man for the Divine.

There have been many attempts to enter and absorb the depth of the Hindu Vedanta and scale the heights of *advaita*. As the Mundaka Upanishad says, "In the farthest sheath abides the Brahma...." Depth is usually associated with descent. But the diary of Swami Abhishiktananda is rightly titled *Ascent to the Depth of the Heart*, because one rises into the luminosity of that beatific vision experienced in the heart of such seekers.

There are striking parallels between Swami Vivekananda and Swami Abhishiktananda: Swami Vivekananda had the vision of Shiva's fiery column at Amarnath. It was an overwhelming experience for him. He survived five years after this experience. In the case of Swami Abhishiktananda too, something similar happened when he suffered a heart attack on the road in Rishikesh. He described it as being burnt by the fiery column of Shiva of Arunachala.

Theologically, the Hindu and Christian traditions can be different. But at the level of spiritual experience, differences dissolve. Swamiji had no problem when he had the ecstatic experience of seeing the fiery column of Shiva. Nor did Ramakrishna Paramahamsa have any theological problems when he had the vision of Christ. Spiritual alchemy is at the heart of any transforming spiritual experience.

Swami Abhishiktananda's favorite mantra was from the Svetasvatara Upanishad:

> I have come to know that mighty Person
> golden like the Sun, beyond all darkness.
> By knowing him a man transcends death,
> there is no other path for reaching that goal. (3:8)

* * *

The assumption that we are allowed to practice only one religion and that the great world religions are mutually exclusive is a quaint notion that will surely become as obsolete as the concept that we should know only one language. The great religions of the world, when taken together, constitute a tremendous reservoir of spiritual and philosophical wisdom, and there is really no good reason why we should confine ourselves only to one of them.

In fact, in Nepal, to take an example, there are many people who practice both Hinduism and Buddhism; while in Japan, the well-known saying goes that people are often born into the Shinto tradition, get married as Christians, and die as Buddhists.

In this connection it must be reiterated that the Hindu–Christian interaction over the past century has been an extremely interesting one. This is highlighted in a remarkable book entitled *Ascent to the Depth of the Heart*, the spiritual diary of Swami Abhishiktananda. He was profoundly impressed by Hinduism, particularly by the *advaita* philosophy of the Upanishads. In the great seer, Sri Ramana Maharshi, he found his guru, and though he remained a Catholic till the end of his life, his remarkable spiritual experiences testify to the fact that the theological differences evaporate when spiritual realization dawns.

Though Hinduism and Christianity have profound theological differences—Hinduism believes in multiple lives until one attains liberation, for example, while Christianity postulates only one life on earth—at a deeper level, such theological differences become insignificant.

As is well known, Sri Ramakrishna Paramahamsa had no theological problem when, in the course of his amazing *sadhana*, he encountered Jesus Christ. For Abhishiktananda too, his experience of the all-pervasive Brahman was overwhelming, even as he held on to his belief in Jesus Christ as a unique savior.

Indeed, the dichotomy between a vast impersonal consciousness and devotion to a personal deity is one that is to be found, to a lesser or greater degree, within every religious tradition. Hinduism has always sought to harmonize the two. This is particularly the case in the Upanishads, which are the high watermark of Hindu philosophy. The Ishavasya Upanishad is an outstanding text on the synthesis between the One and the Many, while in the Svetasvatara Upanishad, Shiva is clearly linked with the *advaitic* consciousness.

It is not possible here to enter into a long debate regarding the *advaita* (unitary) and *dvaita* (dual) consciousness of the Divine. Let it suffice to say that, at the point when spiritual realization is achieved, such theoretical differences would seem to disappear. That certainly is the testimony of saints and mystics belonging to all the world's great religious traditions.

The main point to be noted in this discussion, however, is that spiritual realization cannot take place simply on the intellectual or theoretical plane. It is only when one dives into the depths of the heart—the *hridaya-guhayam*, as the Upanishads have it—that one can hope to transcend verbalization and enter the actual experience.

Let us always remember that the spiritual transmutation is an eternal and ongoing process. As Maulana Jalaluddin Rumi says in his great *Masnavi*:

> Whenever I look there are torches and candles,
> Wherever I turn there is tumult and shouting,
> For the World today is heavy and in travail
> Seeking to give birth to the eternal world.

This interface between the everyday world and the eternal world is at the core of spiritual striving. The great religions of the world provide an outer structure and a systematic paradigm within which the quest can be undertaken; but in the final analysis, the inner spirit is free to follow "the dictates of the heart." This is what the Hindu–Christian monk Swami Abhishiktananda reveals in his moving and deeply reflective *Ascent to the Depth of the Heart*.

NOTES

Introduction

1. The first volume of the MID *Bulletin* appeared in 1977. In October 2005, with issue number 75, the *Bulletin* went to an on-line only format. In January 2011, *Dialogue Interreligieux Monastique*/Monastic Interreligious Dialogue (DIMMID) is planning to launch *Dilatato Corde,* an on-line, international, multilingual periodical. When it appears MID will no longer publish its own *Bulletin.* All past issues, however, will be archived on the DIMMID website.

2. The Abhishiktananda Society began publishing an *Occasional Bulletin,* later known as *SETU,* in November 1975. When the Society was dissolved in 2008, publication ceased. All issues will be archived on the DIMMID website.

An Interview with Odette Baumer-Despeigne

1. "Swamiji" is the respectful title given to a Hindu monk, and his friends and admirers used it for Abhishiktananda.

Early Glimpses of Abhishiktananda

1. She is not to be confused with Sister Thérèse Lemoine, a French Carmelite nun from Lisieux who arrived in India in 1965. After some years at the Carmel in Pondicherry she received an indult of exclaustration and became a hermit.

Pilgrim and Hermit

1. From James Stuart, *Swami Abhishiktananda: His Life Told through His Letters* (Delhi: ISPCK, 1989), p. 213.

2. Abhishiktananda, *Ascent to the Depth of the Heart.* (Delhi: ISPCK, 1998), p. 323 (omitting the Sanskrit words).

3. The expression refers to the title of a book with selections from his writings, edited by Dom André Gozier.

4. 7 December 1973.

5. See, for example, the article by Judson B. Trapnell, "Abhishiktananda's Contemplative Vocation and Contemporary India," *Vidyajyoti: Journal of Theological Reflection* 67, no. 3 (March 2003): 161–179.

Abhishiktananda and the Challenge of Hindu–Christian Experience

1. *Ascent to the Depth of the Heart,* Delhi: ISPCK, 1998.

Enveloped by Mystery

1. Alfredo Marranzini SJ, "Impulse nach Italien," in *Karl Rahner: Bilder eines Lebens,* ed. Paul Imhof and Hubert Biallowons (Zurich and Freiburg: Benzinger and Herder, 1985), p. 104.

2. Karl Rahner, "The Church and Atheism" in *Theological Investigations,* vol. 21 (New York: Crossroad, 1988), p. 148.

3. In *Theological Investigations,* vol. 4 (Baltimore: Helicon, 1966), p. 36.

4. Karl Rahner, "The Church and Atheism," p. 141.

5. *Sagesse hindoue, mystique chrétienne* (Paris: Centurion, 1965); English translation: *Saccidananda: A Christian Approach to Advaitic Experience* (Delhi: ISPCK, 1967); often reprinted and translated into other languages.

6. Henri Le Saux/Abhishiktananda, *La montée au fond du coeur: Le journal intime du moine chrétien-sannyasi,* 1948–73, ed. Raimundo Panikkar (Paris: O.E.I.L., 1986).

7. James Stuart, *Swami Abbishiktananda: His Life Told through His Letters* (Delhi: I.SPCK, 1989).

8. In addition to biographical material in James Stuart's book mentioned above, see also Marie-Madeleine Davy, *Henri Le Saux, Swami Abbishiktananda: Le passeur entre deux rives* (Paris: Les Editions du Cerf, 1981); Odette Baumer-Despeigne, "The Spiritual Journey of Henri Le Saux-Abhishiktananda," in *Cistercian Studies* 18 (1983) 310–29, and Bettina Bäumer,

"Henri Le Saux," in *Grosse Mystiker: Leben und Wirken,* ed. Gerhard Ruhbach and Josef Sudbrack (Munich: C.H. Beck, 1984), pp. 338–54.

9. Henri Le Saux to the novice master at Kergonan, 4 December, 1928, in Stuart, p. 3.

10. Abhishiktananda, *The Secret of Arunachala* (Delhi: ISPCK, 1979), p. 9.

11. Abhishiktananda to his sister, 16 July, 1959, in Stuart, p. 134.

12. On the now widely used typology of exclusivism, inclusivism, and pluralism, see Alan Race, *Christians and Religious Pluralism: Patterns in the Christian Theology of Religions* (Maryknoll NY: Orbis, 1983).

13. Henri Le Saux to Jules Monchanin, 18 August 1947, in Stuart, p. 20.

14. Henri Le Saux to his family, 16 September 1948, in Stuart, p. 32.

15. Abhishiktananda, *The Secret of Arunachala*, p. 9.

16. Abhishiktananda to Marc Chaduc, 23 November 1973, in Stuart, p. 359.

17. Abhishiktananda, *La montée*, p. 43 (entry for 24 March 1952; see also the entry for 31 March 1952).

18. Abhishiktananda to his sister, 7 July 1952, in Stuart, p. 63.

19. A complete list of Abhishiktananda's published and unpublished works can be found in Stuart, pp. 369ff.

20. Abhishiktananda, Introduction to *Saccidananda*, rev. ed., p. xv.

21. Abhishiktananda to Raimon Panikkar, 18 October 1972, in Stuart, p. 312.

22. Abhishiktananda, *La montée*, p. 124 (entry for 2 July 1954. Eighteen years later he took the same position in addressing one of his regular correspondents: "After having wrestled with the Angel for years [cf. Gen. 32:23], I am forced to accept that in practice, *de facto*, the whole so-called Christian approach to the 'mystery' is just one of the approaches. A brilliant and sparkling *lila* of 'the One who sports among the worlds,' the reflection in a given mirror of the *Satyam* who simply IS." (Letter to Raimon Panikkar, 23 December 1972, in Stuart, p. 316).

23. Henri Le Saux/ Swami Abhishiktananda, *The Eyes of Light* (Denville, N.J.: Dimension Books, 1983), p. 43.

24. Abhishiktananda, "The Upanishads and *Advaitic* Experience," in *idem, The Further Shore*, rev. ed. (Delhi: ISPCK, 1984), p. 111.

25. Abhishiktananda to Sister Thérèse Lemoine, 16 January 1973, in Stuart, p. 317.

26. Abhishiktananda, "The Upanishads and *Advaitic* Experience," p. 116.

27. Abhishiktananda to Murray Rogers, 2 September 1973, in Stuart, p. 348.

28. Abhishiktananda, Introduction to *Saccidananda*, rev. ed., p. xiii.

29. Abhishiktananda, "Esseulement," in *idem, Interiorité et révélation: Essais théologiques* (Sisteron: Ed. Présence, 1982), p. 134.

30. Abhishiktananda to Marc Chaduc, 3 June 1972, in Stuart, p. 303.

31. Abhishiktananda to Odette Baumer-Despeigne, 28 May 1972, in Stuart, p. 301.

32. Abhishiktananda to Marc Chaduc, 9 October 1973, in Stuart, p. 354.

33. Abhishiktananda to Marc Chaduc, 26 January 1973, in Stuart, pp. 319–20.

34. Abhishiktananda, *Saccidananda*, rev.ed., p. 200.

35. Abhishiktananda to Marc Chaduc, 12 April 1973, in Stuart, p. 329.

36. Abhishiktananda to Sister Thérèse Lemoine, 14 December 1970, in Stuart, p. 269.

37. Abhishiktananda to his sister Marie-Thérèse, 9 August 1973, in Stuart, p. 346.

38. Abhishiktananda to his sister A.-L. Gugen-Le Saux, 18 April 1969, in Stuart, p. 238.

39. Abhishiktananda to Canon J. Lemarié, 7 November 1954, in Stuart, p. 85.

40. Abhishiktananda, "Sannyasa," in *The Further Shore*, p. 26.

41. Abhishiktananda, "The Upanishads and *Advaitic* Experience," p. 116.

42. Abhishiktananda to Marc Chaduc, 12 April 1973, in Stuart, p. 330.

43. Abhishiktananda to Marc Chaduc, 4 October 1973, in Stuart, p. 353.

44. Abhishiktananda to Sister Sara Grant, 26 January 1971, in Stuart, p. 273.

45. Abhishiktananda, *La montée*, p. 471 (entry for 12 September, 1973).

46. *Ibid.*, p. 452 (entry for late February, 1973).

47. Abhishiktananda to Marc Chaduc, 8 and 11 April 1973, in Stuart, p. 326. In fact, his final illness prevented his going to Delhi at all for these lectures.

48. Abhishikatanda to Odette Baumer-Despeigne, 28 June 1971, in Stuart, p. 278.

49. See John Hick and Paul F. Knitter, eds., *The Myth of Christian Uniqueness: Toward a Pluralistic Theology of Religions* (Maryknoll, N.Y.: Orbis, 1987) and Gavin D'Costa, ed., *Christian Uniqueness Reconsidered: The Myth of a Pluralistic Theology of Religions* (Maryknoll NY: Orbis), 1990.

50. Abhishiktananda to Sister Sara Grant, 5 April 1971, in Stuart, p. 276.

51. For a positive evaluation of that earlier effort, see Wayne Teasdale, "Abhishiktananda's Mystical Intuition of the Trinity," *Cistercian Studies* 18 (1983) 60–75.

52. Abhishiktananda to Mrs. Antonia Fonseca, 4 October 1972, in Stuart, p. 311.

53. Abhishiktananda to Marc Chaduc, 20/21 October 1973, in Stuart, p. 356.

54. Louis Dupré, *Transcendent Selfhood: The Rediscovery of the Inner Life* (New York: Seabury, 1976), p. 104.

55. Abhishiktananda, *La montée*, p. 101 (entry for 27 September 1953).

56. Gordon D. Kaufman, *The Theological Imagination* (Philadelphia: Westminster, 1981), pp. 51–52.

57. Peter Phan, "God as Holy Mystery and the Quest for God-equivalents in Interreligious Dialogue," *Irish Theological Quarterly*, 55 (1989) 286.

58. Abhishiktananda to Sister Thérèse Lemoine, 26 July 1969, in Stuart, p. 241.

59. Abhishiktananda, "Sannyasa," *Further Shore*, p. 14.

60. Abhishiktananda, Introduction to *Saccidananda*, rev. ed., p. xiii.

61. Abhishiktananda to Marc Chaduc, 26 October 1973, in Stuart, p. 358.

62. Abhishiktananda to Sister Marie-Gilberte, OCD, 10 February 1965, in Stuart, p. 189.

Swami Abhishiktananda

1. James Stuart, *Swami Abhishiktananda, His Life Told Through His Letters* (Delhi: I.S.P.C.K. 1989).

2. *Ibid.*, p. 19.

3. See Antony Kalliath, *The Word in the Cave* (New Delhi: Intercultural Publications, 1996), pp. 137ff.

4. Henri Le Saux, *La montée au fond du Coeur, Le journal intime du moine chrétien—sannyasi hindou, 1948–1973* (Paris: O.E.I.L., 1986), p. 47.

5. Ibid., p. 384.

6. Ibid., p. 404.

7. Ibid., p. 467.

8. Ibid., p. 405.

9. Stuart, *op. cit.*, p. 342.

10. Le Saux, *op. cit.*, p. 92.

11. Henri Le Saux, *The Eye of Light* (Rockaway, N.J.: Dimension Books, 1983), p. 69.

12. Le Saux, *La montée au fond du coeur*, p. 101.

13. Stuart, *op. cit.*, p. 207.

14. See Kalliath, *op. cit.*, pp. 337–339.

15. Le Saux, *La montée*, p. 425.

16. See Kalliath, *op. cit.*, pp. 369–371.

17. Stuart, *op. cit.*, p. 275, 307.

18. A. K. Coomaraswamy, *Selected Papers,* Vol. 2, *Metaphysics,* ed. Roger Lipsey (Princeton: Princeton University Press, 1977), p. 8.

19. Frances Young, "The Critic and Visionary," *Scottish Journal of Theology* (Vol. 41:1988):297–312.

20. Thomas Merton, *The Asian Journal of Thomas Merton* (New York: New Direction, 1973), p. 313.

21. John Dunne, *The Way of all the Earth* (New York: Macmillan, 1972), p. ix.

An Introduction to the Diary of Swami Abhishiktanada

1. *Ascent to the Depth of the Heart: The Spiritual Diary of Swami Abhishiktananda (1910–1963),* ed. Raimon Panikkar; trans. David Flemming and James Stuart (Delhi: ISPCK, 1999).

Glossary

Abhiklipta: Integrated, experienced

Abhishiktananda: Bliss of the Anointed One

Advaita: Non-dualism of the Self and the Absolute (*atman* and *Brahman*); central teaching of the Upanishads and of Vedanta.

Aham: I

Aham Asmi: I am

Akasa: Space, infinite, empty space, inner and outer

Akhanda: Undivided

Ahimsa: Not harming; non-violence

Alinga: Without any sign

Ananda: Bliss, beatitude

Anama: Without any name

Anubhava: Experience; mystical experience

Atman: Soul or inner Self, the innermost reality in all

Atmabala: Strength of the Self

Atmakrida: One who sports with the Self

Atmamithunah: One who unites with the Self

Atmananda: One whose delight is in the Self

Avatara: Divine descent; incarnation

Avyakta: Unmanifest

Bhajan: A Hindi devotional song in praise of God

Bhakta: A devotee, a lover of God; a follower of bhakti yoga, the path of love and devotion

Bhakti: Devotion; divine love

Bhaktimarga: The path of devotion

Brahmachari: Celibate; novice

Brahman: The all-pervading Absolute

Cit: Consciousness

Dalit: Member of the suppressed classes of Indian society

Darshana: Vision, view; audience with or seeing the *guru* or deity; philosophy as worldview, Indian system of philosophy

Deha: Body

Dharma: Cosmic law, order, moral and religious duty; teaching; religion

Diksha: Initiation

Epoché: Bracketing out (Greek)

Gnosis: Knowledge (Greek), usually in the sense of higher knowledge

Guha: Cave

Guru: Spiritual teacher

Jyoti: Light

Jivanmukta: One liberated while living; saint

Jnana: Spiritual knowledge or wisdom,

Jnanamarga: The path of knowledge

Karmamarga: Way of action

Kenosis: Emptying (Greek)

Kirtan: Song of praise, singing the divine names

Koinonia: Community (Greek)

Krishna: Avatara of Vishnu, who revealed the Bhagavad Gita (Song of the Lord)

Krita: Made, created

Kshetra: Sacred place, pilgrimage site

Lila: Sport; play

Mahasamadhi: "Great absorption," death of a saint

Maya: Illusion, phenomenal reality or creative power

Metanoia: Conversion; change of mind and heart (Greek)

Mauna: Silence

Murti: Divine image, icon

Namarupa: Names and forms; phenomenal reality

Narayana: Name of the god Vishnu

Neti neti: "Not this, not this," negative theology of the Upanishads

Nirvikalpa: Thought-free

Om: Sacred syllable; most sacred *mantra* in all Indian traditions

Om tat sat: "Om this is that," short formula of the Upanishads, stating the unity of Brahman (*tat*) with Being (*sat*)

Parama: Supreme

Paramarthika: Pertaining to the ultimate level

Parivrajaka: Itinerant monk

Paraspara: Mutual relationship; reciprocity

Prajapati: Creator God; Father of creatures in the Veda

Prana: Breath, life

Pranava: The sacred syllable OM

Purnam: Fullness

Purusha: Cosmic and inner Person, Divine Man

Rama: Avatara of Vishnu, hero of the epic Ramayana

Rsi/Rishi: Poet; sage

Saccidananda: "Being-Consciousness-Bliss," characteristic of Brahman

Sadguru: True Master; God

Sadhana: Spiritual practice

Sadhu: Ascetic, wandering monk

Sahasrara: Yogic center at the crown of the head

Saktinipata: Descent of grace

Samadhi: Meditative state of absorption; burial site of a holy person

Sangam: Confluence of two rivers

Sannyasa: Renunciation, state of life renouncing the world

Sannyasi: Renouncer, Hindu monk

Sat: Being

Satyam: Truth

Shaivism: Religion holding Shiva as the supreme God

Shantivanam: Peace grove, the location of the Saccidananda Ashram

Shiva: Great God (Mahadeva), lit. the gracious One

Sramanas: Traditions of renouncers or monks, as Buddhism and Jainism

Sushupti: Deep sleep

Svayam-jyoti: Self-effulgent light

Swami: Lord, title of a Hindu monk

Swamiji: Honorific appellation of a monk (Sannyasi)

Tantric: Belonging to the tradition of the Tantras (scriptures)

Tat Tvam Asi: "That art thou," one of the great sayings of the Upanishads, stating the identification of the seeker/ disciple with the Absolute (*tat*=Brahman)

Theandric: Divine–human

Upalabdha: Received

Upasana: Meditation; specific forms of meditation in the Upanishads

Vedanta: "End of the Veda," denotes both, the Upanishads as the text group at the end of the Veda, and the philosophical systems developed on this basis, the most prominent being the Advaita Vedanta as advocated by Shankara (eighth century A.D.).

Vidya: Wisdom, knowledge

Visvamaya: Creation as the form of God; immanence

Visvarupa: The Divine whose form is the All; omniform

Vyavaharika: Manifestation; worldly existence

Yoga: "Union," spiritual practice

Yogi: Ascetic, practitioner of Yoga

Fr. William Skudlarek OSB, is a monk of Saint John's Abbey, Collegeville, Minnesota. After serving for five years as president and then executive director of the North American branch of Monastic Interreligious Dialogue, he was appointed General Secretary of *Dialogue Interreligieux Monastique*/Monastic Interreligious Dialogue in September 2007. In addition to having taught theology and homiletics at Saint John's University, he served as a Maryknoll Associate in Brazil and was a member of Saint John's Abbey's priory in Japan. During his years in Japan he began to practice zazen with the Sanbô Kyôdan. He is the author of *Demythologizing Celibacy: Practical Wisdom from Christian and Buddhist Monasticism* (Liturgical Press, 2008), and coeditor of *Green Monasticism: A Buddhist–Catholic Response to an Environmental Calamity* (Lantern Books, 2010).

Of Related Interest from Lantern Books

The Spiritual Life
A Dialogue of Buddhist and Christian Monastics
Edited by Donald W. Mitchell and James A. Wiseman

Finding Peace in Troubled Times
Buddhist and Christian Monastics on Transforming Suffering
Edited by Donald W. Mitchell and James A. Wiseman

Green Monasticism
A Buddhist-Catholic Response to an Environmental Calamity
Edited by Donald W. Mitchell and William Skudlarek

Islam Is...
An Experience of Dialogue and Devotion
Mary Magaret Funk

The Common Heart
An Experience of Interreligious Dialogue
Netanel Miles-Yepez

Order from www.lanternbooks.com or 1.703.661.1500

Breinigsville, PA USA
17 May 2010
238178BV00001B/2/P